BE THAT UNICORN

PRAISE FOR *BE THAT UNICORN*

"Sometimes being a unicorn is lonely. After all, we're pretty unique creatures. Jenny Block teaches us all how to embrace our inner unicorn, let our magic shine, and find our herd!"

> —Desiree Asher, philanthropist, technologist, unicorn

"This book is a valuable guide to have by your side as you make the tough calls, keep the culture positive, and take a little time to reflect on your own inner unicorn."

> —Carrie Welch, cofounder of Feast Portland and Little Green Pickle

"Jenny brings a magical energy to every room she's in and people notice. *Be That Unicorn* reveals her journey of becoming her authentic, wonderful self. Thank you for sharing your magic, Jenny."

> —Celebrity chef Duff Goldman, founder of Charm City Cakes and star of Food Network's *Ace of Cakes*

"We need Jenny Block and *Be That Unicorn*, her wry, insightful, poignant, and hilarious guide to discovering and harnessing the magic that lives inside of all of us and that, when unleashed, allows us to be our very best—and most authentic—selves."

> —Noah Michelson, editorial director of HuffPost Personal

"*Be That Unicorn* has a lot of valuable tips, that even That Unicorn may forget sometimes. It's a good read that everyone should have the pleasure of picking up."

> —Maddie Whitley, trans model and activist

BE THAT UNICORN

Find Your Magic, Live Your Truth, and Share Your Shine

JENNY BLOCK

mango
PUBLISHING

CORAL GABLES

Published by Mango Publishing Group, a division of Mango Media Inc.

Cover Design: Liz Hong
Author photo credit: © Lisa Hause, Lisa Hause Photography •
lisahausephotography.com
Unicorn Watercolors Credit: © Suzanne L. Vinson • suzannelvinson.com
Layout & Design: Morgane Leoni

For permission requests, please contact the publisher at:
Mango Publishing Group
2850 S Douglas Road, 2nd Floor
Coral Gables, FL 33134 USA
info@mango.bz

For special orders, quantity sales, course adoptions and corporate sales, please email the publisher at sales@mango.bz. For trade and wholesale sales, please contact Ingram Publisher Services at customer.service@ingramcontent.com or +1.800.509.4887.

Be That Unicorn: Find Your Magic, Live Your Truth, and Share Your Shine

Library of Congress Cataloging-in-Publication number: 2019948837
ISBN: (print) 978-1-64250-184-1, (ebook) 978-1-64250-185-8
BISAC category code SEL023000—SELF-HELP / Personal Growth / Self-Esteem

Printed in the United States of America

For Papa Herbie.

My papa and my unicorn.

CONTENTS

———

PREFACE

I've always wanted to be that "It Girl." The one people were drawn to. The one who could garner the attention of everyone at a dinner party. The one who was so captivating that, no matter where she was or who she was talking to, everyone around her just glowed. The "It Girl" has some sort of magic force about her, and just being around her allowed you to become enveloped in it.

I used to think you became an "It Girl" through clothes or beauty or money. Maybe it was her travel or her experiences or her access to the world. The messaging from that world is confusing. "Be rich. Be young. Be beautiful. Then everyone will love you and you'll have the world at your feet." But some of the most banal people I have ever met get top marks in all three of those categories. So it sent me out on a journey pondering, "If that wasn't what made the girl—or the guy— what was it?"

It wasn't until I truly listened to the words my father had been saying to me since I was a little girl that I realized what the magic quotient of the It Girl truly was: authenticity. She feels so comfortable in her skin that she can't help but let it spring out from her like so many sparkly strands that surround and delight everyone around her.

Because she feels good about herself, she makes others feel the same way. There's no one easier to adore than someone who reflects back to you the image of yourself that you long to see: the smart, funny, clever, enchanting, kind, calm, inviting version of yourself that knows just what to do and how to do it in every situation.

That girl (or guy) is That Unicorn.

I used to get angry when my dad would tell me to be myself. That plan had gotten me rejected in the most grandiose of ways, including when I went to Camp Louise the summer between eighth and ninth grades. Everyone else had grown up and arrived at camp with luggage packed with Bloomies underwear and magazine pages to hang in their lockers of the latest hunky movie stars. I showed up with my monkey puppet: "Hi! I'm Jenny and this is my monkey, Henry." It was social suicide at first sight.

But what I didn't know back then was that those girls were even more insecure than I was. It was that very desperation that pushed them to follow the crowd in every sense, to dress the same and talk the same and drool over the very same heartthrobs. I was too naïve to know any better. I was just being, well, me. That summer was the beginning of me deciding that that whole "be yourself" thing was for the birds. All it got you was a seat at the dork table in the cafeteria and a lot of lonely Saturday nights.

But years of following the crowd did me no good, either. Not in the long run, anyway. Why? Because I wasn't being me. I was faking it...and not in the "fake it till you make it" kind of way, just in the plain old "fake it 'cause you don't know what the heck else to do" kind of way. That's never good. When *I* was faking it, I *felt* fake. When I was my actual self, I felt so much better. Slowly it became clear to me: being yourself might not always be the easiest, but it is always the best.

So, when I got to college, I decided it was the perfect time to retest my dad's "be yourself and they will come" theory. And, go figure, it worked. People liked to be around me because I knew who I was and I was happy and comfortable in my own skin. From then on, that was my path. Sure, I had and continue to have plenty of days plagued by insecurity. But most days are pretty prancy. I became That Unicorn by not *trying* to be any girl other than me.

That Unicorn is the best you. That Unicorn is a glittery, rainbow-maned metaphor for one's joyful self...the kind of person we are all drawn to. That Unicorn is *you*. My mom has always said that people are drawn to me because I make everyone feel good about themselves. Throughout my life, people have echoed that sentiment. It's the thing I love about myself the most: I'm the big sister, the BFF, the mom, the cheerleader, the coach..."the little unicorn that could" who everyone deserves.

The truth is, we are all unicorns seeking to be heard and to be a part of the herd. It's really that simple. Remember that, and things that never made sense before will suddenly click. Trust me.

People tell me that I make them want to be themselves; they see how there is nothing wrong with honoring all of the different parts that make up who you are and doing your best to smile along the way as you do. People do often ask me, "Do you always smile?" Not always, I tell them, but most of the time. Because, even if I'm not experiencing joy right at that moment, I still want everyone around me to experience it.

The thing is, in every situation, we have the opportunity to prance or to plop. To prance is to keep on keeping on, hopefully with a smile on your face. To plop is when you just say "okay" to what you're given or told. It's resignation.

I do my very best to just keep prancing. Sure, I could choose the path of least resistance. I could remain seated, stay quiet, let any old obstacle stop me in my tracks. Or I could choose to *just keep at it*. Perhaps with a grimace at first, but eventually with a smile.

You don't even have to be anyone special to make this work. This is an "act as if" kind of proposition. You act as if you are just pleased as punch to leap another hurdle and, somehow, you find you *are* pleased as punch...if not about all the hurdle-leaping, then at least the success you achieved because of it.

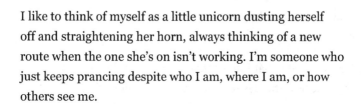

I like to think of myself as a little unicorn dusting herself off and straightening her horn, always thinking of a new route when the one she's on isn't working. I'm someone who just keeps prancing despite who I am, where I am, or how others see me.

That Unicorn doesn't let anyone else define her. That Unicorn creates her own path and does it with love and kindness and respect. And That Unicorn leaves a little sparkle wherever she goes so that others have a chance to follow.

At its core, being That Unicorn is about being yourself and feeling really, really good about that and making others feel really, really good about themselves too. It's all about contradictions and not following the crowd or doing the expected. *That Unicorn* knows that, to lead a unicorn life, you have to find your magic, live your truth, and always share your shine.

Note: These days, authors have to make some choices when it comes to pronouns. I chose singular feminine (she/her) pronouns for That Unicorn because I personally use she/her to refer to myself.

Being That Unicorn is about being true to yourself. So, I am practicing what I preach. This isn't meant to exclude or offend—anyone can be a unicorn! Thank you for understanding.

CHAPTER ONE

What Does It Mean to Be That Unicorn?

(In Other Words...How to BTU While Living)

I like to think of myself as being That Unicorn. I also have an inner unicorn. His name is Herbert—Herbie for short. That was my papa's name. Papa died on Valentine's Day in 1988, and he was also a unicorn. He found his magic, lived his truth, and shared his shine. Oh, how he shared it. You could not be around him, not even for a moment, without feeling all the love. I tell everyone I was his favorite grandchild, but I believe he made each of his grandchildren feel like his favorite. He came to every rehearsal for every play I ever did. He took me out to breakfast at the Ideal Diner, just him and me, before anyone else in the house woke up. And he always gave me a little bit of cash. "A person needs some walking-around money," he would tell me.

On the way to his funeral, I swear I saw him standing on the corner, wearing the hat with the feather in it and a string tie, jingling the change in his pocket. He nodded at me. "You got this, kid," I imagined him saying. I hear him say that in my head every time I need a little push.

Papa was sad sometimes. Undiagnosed depression, I imagine. He would sit alone now and again, eyes closed, lost in his thoughts. But after he had some time to "rest his eggies," as he would say, he would put on his hat and motion to the door: "Let's get out of here." Then he would take me on one sort of adventure or another. Papa was my hero. Herbert is my unicorn. Everyone needs an inner unicorn.

Being That Unicorn isn't about being perfect. It isn't about glossing over the hard stuff or the sad stuff. It's about being true to yourself and not letting life hold you down, because it certainly will try. The only real magic in the world is the magic you will find inside your own head. You can use it to hold you up and propel you forward and to help others to do the same. You use it when you feel like you just can't.

"Herbert, we've got to wrangle this," I whisper in my own ear, and away we go. Sometimes, I imagine him carrying me into battle. It's a silly image, I suppose. But I kind of love it. It makes me smile and it gives me that little push I need to do the things that of course I can do, despite fearing that I can't.

You don't have to name your unicorn. Ultimately, your unicorn is you. But it helps me to feel like I have an ongoing partner in crime. It means I'm never alone. Herbert is my spirit guide, my magic feather, my Jiminy Cricket, my inner voice. To be That Unicorn is to heed that whisper that never falters. The magic is in discovering and trusting what you're hearing, that consistent message that says you are amazing.

You *are* amazing...and yet things are still going to get messed up now and again. Here's the difference between unicorns and everyone else: That Unicorn knows it's worth picking up the pieces. What's the other choice anyway? Wallowing? That's no fun and so very unproductive. And that's not the person we look up to and long to be. It just isn't. We long to be the person who walks through life horn up, not horn down. Who doesn't ignore the puddles, but instead puts on her boots and jumps through them. Who doesn't leave others in the muck, but leads the way around the mess. Who treats others the way she wants to be treated, not for gain but simply (as my wife likes to say) because it's the right thing to do.

That Unicorn knows that the natural enemy of life is becoming overwhelmed. When we get overwhelmed, we lose sight of what we wanted in the first place. That Unicorn is an ace at keeping her eye on the prize. To live like That Unicorn is the ultimate goal. The good news is, we don't have to be perfect at it. The great news is, with our inner unicorn as our guide, we just might have a chance at doing a pretty darn good job of it.

All day long and from every angle, we hear what we should be doing, how we should be doing it, and what we should look like while we're at it. Most of what is thrown at us is preposterously unattainable. Much of it is about giving our money to companies who care very little about us but a whole lot about making money. Life is a much shorter trip than you might think. My dad says to think of it as an amusement park to which you can only ever get one ticket, and, once it's closed, it's closed. You have one chance to ride the rides and see the shows and taste the cotton candy and connect with the other people there.

You can waste your time being afraid—afraid you'll look silly on the ride, worried you won't laugh at the right parts of the show, stressed you'll throw up from the cotton candy, scared that, if you wait in line for this ride, then the line for the other might get too long. You can live in fear, and you can miss it all. Or you can go for it. You can trust that you know best what you can do, what you want to do, and what you can handle. And you go for it. I know that I don't want to spend my life sitting on the bench. I know because I used to do exactly that.

I used to be the coat and drinks and backpack holder. Whatever the activity, I held down the fort with everyone's things while everyone else enjoyed the day. One afternoon, I was at Walt Disney World with my best friend and my then seven-year-old daughter, standing in line for Splash Mountain. We had just reached the "point of no return," which is where I planned to duck out. But before I stepped out of line, I looked to my right and there it was: the mommy bench. There sat the saddest-looking mommies at Disney, covered with snotty, crying kids crawling on their pitiful-looking moms draped in already discarded souvenirs and acetate costumes. And to my left was a line full of kids and adults alike, talking and laughing and all excited to go on the ride. The life metaphor simply could not be denied.

I decided to go on that ride. And, you know what? It was really fun. And I wondered in that moment about the things

I had missed and the things I would continue to miss. That initiated The Year of Yes. And that first year led to many more years, which led to learning to ski and rock-climb, rappelling down the façade of an eighteen-story hotel, feeding sharks and diving with octopi, and a list of a zillion other wild and even not-so-wild things. I gave up the bench and decided to grab hold of that one-day-only ticket and, well, live. That was the day my unicorn journey really took off in earnest.

That Unicorn knows how to live.

When it comes to living, That Unicorn acknowledges that...

Social media is bogus.

It is. All of it. No, really. Not some of it. All of it. Even the most uncurated post is still curated. The picture was *taken*, right? The post was *written*, right? And either one or both got posted, right? Those acts in and of themselves were executed, even if subconsciously. The photo was taken to post or *with posting in mind*. The subject, the angle, the light, all of it was curated. The words were written specifically for posting. Each word chosen for others to read and approve of and comment on.

Social media is fake. It's not about connecting us or bringing us together. It's not about sharing. If it were, it would look totally different. And, sure, it *can* connect us. But that's not its purpose. What it really serves to do is precisely what its unfortunate roots set out to do—to judge and compare people. It started out as hot or not. Now it's hot or not...plus wealthy or not, successful or not, married or not, traveling or not. You get the idea.

So, That Unicorn knows that social media is nothing more than a game. If you feel like playing and you can do it without getting hurt or depressed by remembering that it's not real, no harm, no foul. But social media is not a forced march. You can choose not to use it. You can check in occasionally to see what friends and family are up to. There is not a thing in the world wrong with that. That Unicorn knows who she is and doesn't need a post or quote or quiz to prove it.

No unicorn's life is perfect.

It might seem like there are unicorns who have it all, especially celebrities and the super-rich. But too many of them aren't actually unicorns. They're more like robots, with someone else doing all their thinking while they live in a shell to keep people from getting too close to them. And their "perfect" lives are what we see on TV or in a magazine (or in their Instagram feed). We know nothing of their real lives, their real struggles. Sure, their struggles may be more glamorous than most of ours are. But very few of them have what you or I would consider a perfect life.

They can't go anywhere without people taking their photo or asking to speak to them. They have someone controlling their every move in the name of furthering their careers. They must watch their Ps and Qs to not end up in a tabloid or get kicked out of this club or that group. They aren't their own person. They are beholden to the money or the work. Wealth and celebrity have perks—and some pretty damn good ones for sure—but those things have their burdens as well.

Part of being a unicorn is dealing with what some might consider imperfections. Jobs and families and bodies and relationships that sometimes drive us crazy. And yet, we are who we are. We have made the lives we want to live with what we have been given. That Unicorn does her personal best, no more and no less. That's different for every unicorn. And the end game isn't perfection, it's living honestly.

Perfect is never the goal.

"Perfect" according to whom? Who gets to decide? And what's the reward for meeting that arbitrary standard? Neither answer matters, because perfect doesn't exist. Unless you're talking about *your* perfect, in which case, that qualifier is absolutely required. That Unicorn is seeking the life that's perfect for her. She doesn't ask anyone's permission or need anyone's approval when it comes to what that looks like or how she gets there.

"Perfect" often gets in the way of "pretty darn good." It keeps us focused on what *isn't* real, which forces us to miss what *is*. Will that more expensive car or bigger house or fancier dress make us *that* much happier? Maybe for a minute. But in the long run, That Unicorn is so much more about being happy than about battling windmills in the pursuit of the elusive perfect that she can't be bothered with the little things that are mere distractions along the way.

Since there is no perfect, having that as a goal leads to failure. Unicorns are looking for *their* perfect. They're looking for perfectly *them*. They're seeking That Unicorn in the mirror, looking back at them with that knowing smile, telling them, "You're doing great because you're doing you."

Sometimes, no matter what, everything falls apart.

This is a hard one, even for That Unicorn. Sometimes everything goes to pieces, and there's just not much good to be found. People get sick. The house floods. Jobs are lost. Bills pile up. Kids get in trouble. Nothing is going right. It's not good. But it is real and it does have to be wrangled and it will end.

That Unicorn doesn't need to be told to find the silver lining. Sometimes there really isn't one. That Unicorn doesn't need to be told "Keep your chin up" or "At least you're better off than some people" or "At least you have (fill-in-the-blank)." That Unicorn knows that there are times when the universe—at least hers—comes terribly unglued, and the only way out is through. And so first, unicorns allow themselves to scream and cry and kick and bemoan the unfairness of it all. And then...

Then That Unicorn says, "This has to be done. And I am the one who has to do it." And she does it. That's why we long to be That Unicorn so much. It's not that unicorns are unaffected by the world; it's that they don't let it change their paths. It's not that they never face a storm; it's that they go in wearing their foul-weather gear and armed with umbrellas. It's not that they don't get sad or mad or disappointed; it's that they don't let it stop them. And don't think you have to smile through it all, either. Sometimes unicorns grit their teeth, too.

Nobody really has it all figured out.

That's the big secret. I hope it doesn't scare you to hear that. What I hope instead is that it makes it all the more clear to you how within reach being a unicorn is. That Unicorn looks like she knows it all because she moves through the world without anything stopping her, not because she knows everything, but because she knows she can figure it out or find it out.

Too many people wait to do something until they are sure the conditions are ideal. Enough time together to move in, enough experience to apply for that job, enough time to take that class, enough background to ask that question. The problem is, it could feel like it's never enough. Then, before you know it, the moment is long past.

Unicorns aren't thoughtless. But they don't wait indefinitely, either. They're not entitled, but they also know their worth. They aren't afraid to tell you that they're ready, even though they wonder in the middle of the night if they are. Unicorns leap. They take calculated risks. They trust themselves. They are confident enough in their own unicorn-ness to know that yes is the answer even when insecurity threatens their confidence. That Unicorn takes the chance; otherwise, That Unicorn knows, she has no chance.

Wanting more is okay.
So is not wanting more.

There's nothing wrong with wanting the corner office or the biggest piece of cake. There's nothing wrong with wanting to star in the play or be the best at cruise karaoke. There's nothing wrong with wanting the promotion or being known as the best baker in the neighborhood. There's nothing wrong with wanting more. It's not un-unicorn to want more.

It's also okay *not* to want more. There's nothing in the world wrong with the path you choose. Don't let anyone put a "just" in front of your life. "Oh, you just stay at home with the kids." "You just do volunteer work, right?" "So, you just freelance?" Those people are speaking to their own insecurities; they define themselves by their work. That's their stuff, not yours.

That Unicorn knows how much is enough for her: how much work, how much play, how much money. It's not up to other people to define that for you. Anyone who tries is merely wrangling with their own demons, and no unicorn has time for that. It's not selfish to want more, and it's not pitiful to be happy where you are. It's just sad that we go around judging one another on these make-believe things when there is a perfectly good gauge of unicorns and humans—kindness, especially to the smallest and most powerless among us...

7 Unicorns ask for help.

Asking for help is good. Accepting help is divine. There is very little in life where we don't benefit from asking for help. I think it's a shame that we often feel that, unless we did it all on our own, it's not worthy of credit or celebration. When we're growing up, we hear an awful lot of, "Good for you. You got dressed all by yourself." "Look at you! You brushed your teeth without any help!" "What a big girl you are—you finished your homework all on your own." It is a rite of passage to be able to do certain things for ourselves that a healthy, able-bodied child (and later a healthy, able-bodied adult) should be able to do alone. Autonomy is important.

But doing something alone is not more important than the actual doing. If you need help, ask for it. I'm tiny: I could never take luggage on a plane if I didn't ask for help putting it in the overhead compartment. Heck, I couldn't even grocery shop alone without some assistance—I wouldn't be able to get any of the products on my list that reside on the highest shelves. It's great to be able to do things for yourself, but don't let it define you.

No unicorn would ever expect people to do things for her. Entitlement is exceptionally unbecoming of a unicorn. But asking politely is not just acceptable, it's also part of being in community. Most people actually like to help. When we are open to asking for help, we are also providing the opportunity to help. I love to be called on for things I am able to assist with. It allows me to contribute. Asking, accepting, giving, and receiving help are all integral to being part of a community. That Unicorn never forgets that many of the most significant human accomplishments were not done alone.

A shared life is the best life.

It doesn't matter if it's a significant other or a best friend or a relative. Life's moments are often better when they are shared. It is almost as if you can experience things more robustly when you experience them with someone else. You have your experience, but you also get to watch the person you are with having the experience. You get to talk about the experience, both in the moment and after, and relive it.

That's not to say that there's anything wrong with doing things on your own. There is a great deal to be learned when you take things on all by yourself. But with all of life's highs and lows, sorrows and joys, excitement, and even simplicity, the act of sharing enhances. It can ease the difficult ones as well. Sometimes, it almost feels as if something isn't real unless you have someone there to witness it with and for you.

Humans are pack animals. They are meant to live in groups. They are intended to care for one another and to be cared for. There are certainly people who thrive alone. But most of us find that sharing life and all of its ups and downs with other people is a happier, more fulfilling, and even healthier way to live. It's okay to want to interact with people. It's okay to want to be in the company of others and not interact. And it's okay to spend time recharging solo. That Unicorn knows what she needs and when she needs it, and she shares herself, her life, and her time accordingly.

There's no do-over.

Since I was a little girl, my dad has consistently reminded me that "life is not a dress rehearsal." You only get to do this life-thing once, at least as far as any of us know. Too many of us treat our lives as if we will have another opportunity to do and see and experience the things that we encounter. But this is it, the big show. We don't get a second chance to say yes instead of no, sit in the front of the roller coaster instead of the back, or say hello instead of sitting alone at that table. That Unicorn knows to open the door—or at least look through the peephole—when opportunity comes knocking.

Change can be frightening and challenging. But that is only because it represents the new and unknown. Sure, you're comfortable with where you are and who you're with and what you're doing. And unicorns do love to be comfy. But That Unicorn also knows that she only gets one shot at being her sparkly best, and she owes it to herself, not to say the universe, to take a chance and make things happen and live... really live. The sidelines are safe. But you may never get the same opportunity to take the stage or hit the field or test the waters again. That Unicorn was made to shine.

Life is about singularities. It's made up of a zillion little moments that come and go. When we miss those moments, they are gone forever. So, unless you're going to die or lose your life savings or put others' lives or well-being at risk, climb it, sail it, eat it, sing it, see it, try it, do it. You will likely never be in that moment again. And most of us will have far greater regret about the things we didn't do than about the things we did.

10 Regret serves no one.

Regret is an easy trap to fall into. You don't seize the opportunity presented, and you carry that regret like a millstone around your neck. It weighs you down and follows you around. Ultimately, regret keeps you from seizing the next opportunity, and the next, until you find yourself filled with more regret than satisfaction when it comes to your life and your choices about that life. That's the kind of self-defeating mayhem for which That Unicorn has no time or energy.

Sometimes we do things we're not entirely proud of or thrilled about. We drink a little too much at the party, we say something that hurts someone's feelings, or we don't go on the trip or take the job. It's okay to be disappointed in a choice...for a moment. It's not okay to let that choice ruin you. It doesn't make any sense. Why have one regret compound itself into a zillion more?

That Unicorn is all about living and learning. Don't let one misstep keep you from saying yes to the next opportunity. Instead of regretting a slip, learn from it. Use that mistake to inform how you will act when the next event or trip or job presents itself. You cannot change the past nor predict the future. You can, however, be present in the now and seize every moment that each day gives you. That Unicorn lives with eyes and arms and heart wide open and ready to receive the gifts that—trust me—the universe is designed to offer you. Yesterday is in the books. But today is all yours.

CHAPTER TWO

How to BTU When **Planning**

Unicorns are planners. They have to be. There's too much life to go at it unplanned. But they are also realistic and flexible... just not *too* realistic and not *too* flexible. That's the best part about That Unicorn. She is all the things that we sometimes think are too hard to be. When we plan like That Unicorn, we remember to pack extra socks just in case. But only one pair because a heavy suitcase is the worst. That Unicorn listens to the weather report but always keeps an umbrella in the car; she also knows that wherever you travel, they always sell umbrellas somewhere. That Unicorn knows that to plan is human, but to throw that plan out the window can also be divine.

I've burned myself in both directions—both over-planning and under-planning—so I know what it is to walk the not-so-unicorn path. But I learned from those trips to always go the way of the unicorn. I planned a Disney trip within an inch of its life. No one was ever hangry or over-tired. No one got too hot. Every ride was ridden. Every show was seen. There was park time, pool time, and hotel time. Money was saved. Convenience was had. And there wasn't one fight or meltdown, even though three adults and one five-year-old were involved and staying in one room. It wasn't easy. And all the planning was on me. But it was so worth it.

That Unicorn knows that a good plan means she'll be happy and so will everyone else. Now, others have to be willing to *follow* the plan, and it's a good idea to chart a course where the only person being disadvantaged will be the one *not* following the plan. But, in general, a good plan goes a long way. Proper planning can be a thankless job, but I like to think of everything going smoothly as my reward.

I don't always plan. Sometimes that still works out fine. Sometimes I'm sorry that I didn't plan better. I miss a museum or waste time or resources. I try not to beat myself up about it (even though it's one of the most significant issues I seem to always be working on), and I try to learn for next time. Sometimes, others do the planning. As long as they're good at, I say, "Have at it." And, if it turns out to be a disaster, I chalk it up to experience and make a note not to follow that person's planning again.

The point is, with a plan, life has less of a chance of just passing you by. Plan to get things done, so you're free when your friends are in town. Google restaurants before your road trip so you don't miss the best BBQ on Route 66. Ask for how-to tips about almost anything, and don't waste your time reinventing the wheel. That Unicorn is all about being calm and efficient because calm and efficient always feels better than harried and disorganized.

When it comes to planning, That Unicorn acknowledges that...

Unicorns plan.

That Unicorn doesn't like to leave things that need to be done hanging in the breeze. That's not to say unicorns aren't procrastinators. I certainly am. But even when it seems like I'm leaving something until the bitter end, I still have a plan lined up for getting it done. Unicorn planning is about preparing in a way that works for you.

Here's the thing. That Unicorn is thoughtful—as in, she's full of thoughts. If she doesn't plan—and planning includes writing that plan down!—her brain will be so full of strategies that she won't ever be able to get anything done. One of the best parts about having a plan is that you can then set your mind at ease. There is so much less to worry about when there is a road map in place. Even if things don't go as expected, even if all or much of that plan ends up being scrapped, that plan will still serve as a jumping-off point for whatever it is that needs to happen or get done.

Virtually every aspect of life and virtually every person in your life can benefit from planning. That Unicorn likes to feel like she's in control, rather than drifting through the unknown— that requires planning. How detailed the plan ends up is totally up to you and your comfort level. Maybe it's just a list. Perhaps it's a spreadsheet. Maybe it's a whole notebook with every phone number and address and map. And, likely, it's different depending on what is being planned for.

Unicorns are flexible. But not **too** flexible.

Plans change. That Unicorn understands that and is always ready to adjust. She isn't attached to the plan for its own sake. What she is attached to is getting it done, whatever "it" is. So, if things need to shift, so be it. Of course, That Unicorn is not a pushover. Plans also don't have to be changed just for the sake of changing them.

That Unicorn stands her ground when she's confident that her plan is the best option. She doesn't throw blueprints to the wind just because someone else would prefer to take the reins, especially if that person was nowhere to be found during the planning stages. Non-unicorns like to be the boss of things and think they can do it by winging it. Winging it *can* work. Planning *always* works.

Because not everyone is focused on being That Unicorn, flexibility is key. Otherwise, you don't end up being That Unicorn; you end up being that stick-in-the-mud with no ability to change. Planning serves as the foundation. From that springboard, the situation has to be assessed as things progress. Flexibility means being able to work together with unicorns and non-unicorns and get the job, trip, project, event, or whatever done and done well, without losing your mind or sacrificing the integrity of what needs to get done.

Unicorns rely on reinforcements.

No unicorn is an island. I repeat: *no unicorn is an island*. Just because you are doing all the prep work doesn't mean you have to do all of the executing as well. Even if you have to do the work or travel or whatever alone, that doesn't mean you can't reach out to the people around you to help you execute your plan.

Call your dog-sitter or ask your neighbor or hire a friend. Trade to-dos with someone else who has a plan of their own with which they could use a hand. One of the most significant issues people have with trying to accomplish something is thinking they have to go it alone. One of the best parts of planning ahead is the fact that you can brainstorm who you can bring in to help you to make things work.

Being That Unicorn is about being self-aware enough to know what you are good at and what you are and are not capable of. Being a good planner is based on that kind of self-awareness. There is no shame in calling in the troops. But it would certainly be a shame to have an entire trip or project or whatever go down the drain because you didn't pose the very straightforward question: can you give me a hand?

 ## Unicorns ask questions and do their research.

Planning is not about hiding in a hole and making things up when you don't know how to tackle what's being presented. The best unicorns are the ones who always know someone who they can reach out to get their questions answered. Having the internet is like having every possible expert at the tip of your fingers. Of course, it also means you have every possible person who *thinks* he's an expert at the tip of your fingers. So check your sources and use them wisely.

If you're planning a trip, reach out to a friend who has done a similar trip recently or seek out recent articles in respected publications, online or in print. Looking for a job, going to (or back to) school, baking a cake, crafting, building something, organizing an event: you name it, there's help out there.

Planning is about researching. Even something as simple as creating a timeline to get something done can benefit from research. Find out how long specific steps generally take, and you'll have a much better idea of how to plan your time. The quantity of information available to us can be overwhelming.

But, if you use it wisely, it can be the key to virtually any kind of planning.

Unicorns have a Plan B. And maybe even a Plan C and D.

Sometimes you have to be so flexible that you scrap nearly all of your plan, and, if you're like me, the thought is terrifying. Having an alternate plan means you don't have to worry if things go a little sideways.

Those back-up plans don't have to be as exhaustive as Plan A. A secondary strategy can be as simple as an alternate restaurant or hotel, a second available day or time, a replacement companion or emergency contact—anything that will keep things leading to your end game, even if the path there is an alternate one.

That Unicorn finds comfort in planning, so if planning is making you crazy, you're going too far. Trust me. Excellent planning (including great Plan B planning) can be about little more than lists. But they are lists that keep your mind from spinning and allow you to use your brainpower for fun stuff instead.

Unicorns expect disaster.

They say you can't plan for the unexpected. I don't think that's entirely true. You might not be able to prepare for the specific issue that might arise, but you can plan how you will respond if something comes up. For example, if something dramatically interrupts the plan, I can also call so-and-so, go to (fill-in-the-blank), reschedule, or the like.

The thing you can always count on is something that you didn't count on happening, especially if kids or animals or weather or travel are involved. Unless the only thing the plan needs is you, you should be prepared to welcome disaster like an old friend.

When you expect something to throw you off course, it will surprise you how much less it actually does disrupt you. Sure, there are disasters from which there is no recovery. Some plans get obliterated. There are situations where nothing is what it was supposed to be, and all is basically lost. But those things are outliers. That Unicorn is ready for anything short of that.

Unicorns know it's not about the plan.

That Unicorn always remembers that the plan is the means and not the end. It's that attachment thing again. If you are too attached to the plan, you lose sight of the end game, and you have a far better chance of ending up woefully disappointed. But if you remember that the plan is just a plan, you are sure to fare far better.

A plan is supposed to be comforting. But if the plan starts lording itself over you, it loses its usefulness. You have to be the plan's boss. No exceptions. If you hear yourself saying to yourself, "But the plan said…" even though things are moving along swimmingly outside of what you planned for, then the plan is bossing you, and that is no good.

Planning is a tool—nothing more, nothing less. Do as much or as little, in whatever manner, as suits you. That Unicorn never lets a plan stand in the way. She always remembers that the plan's role is to help. Once it fails to do that, it has to be discarded. Hence, the need for flexibility and a Plan B…

Unicorns trust other unicorns.

That is, they trust those who are better at whatever the thing at hand is. In this case, planning. You can be That Unicorn and not be a great planner. That Unicorn knows when to plan, when to trust another unicorn to plan, and which unicorn that should be. The key is that it needs to be someone better at planning the thing than you. If they aren't, handing over the reins isn't helpful.

This is a common mistake made by That Unicorn because she is so careful of other people's feelings. But That Unicorn knows that she can't give in to others if it is to their detriment. She can still be kind about it. But she doesn't have to sign up to follow the plans of someone who doesn't know the first thing about planning, or about the travel, task, or event at hand.

Trust is vital. That includes trusting yourself and your inner unicorn instincts to know when to trust someone else with the build or the day or the event, and when to say, "Thank you for offering. But I've got this." You are always allowed to say, "I've got this," because I'm quite confident that you do.

Unicorns are humble.

When you're That Unicorn, or you have become good at planning, it can be easy to start thinking too much of yourself, which is a dangerous trap. That Unicorn is equal parts self-confident and humble. Not everyone can manage that feat, which is one of the reasons why they are such a unicorn.

Being humble can actually serve you far better than you may think. When you are humble, people are willing to help you plan, or do anything else for that matter. If you're not so humble, it's easy for others to think, "Well, if she's so great, she can do it herself." That sort of attitude doesn't serve anyone in the end.

Being That Unicorn is about knowing yourself, and a unicorn knows she is great, but also that she is no greater than any other unicorn. Unicorns are different, and they are the same in so many, many ways. But she is never superior. (Except perhaps to someone who is purposely cruel and deceitful and self-serving. There are bad seeds out there, and there's nothing wrong with acknowledging that and keeping them as far from your magical world as possible.)

10 That Unicorn keeps her eyes on the prize.

This can be really hard. Planning can be a pain in the backside—all the research, asking for help, making lists, and packing or buying or prepping or whatever. But That Unicorn works hard to not get bogged down by the process because that's all it is, a process.

Knowing what the result will be and staying focused on that can make the planning stages a heck of a lot easier. Think of it as whistling while you work or taking a spoonful of sugar to make the medicine go down. The end goal isn't the tune or the sweets. What has to be planned for in the meantime is just how you're going to get there.

That Unicorn is a planner because, when it comes right down to it, planning is the only way to go, and keeping what you're planning for at the front of your mind can help you keep your horn up when you're slogging through. This too shall pass, and we shall all be the better for it!

CHAPTER THREE

——

How to BTU When **Working**

Perhaps the hardest place to be That Unicorn is at work. Even if you're one of the lucky ones who love their jobs, work is hard. Otherwise, as the saying goes, it wouldn't be work. But not allowing yourself to be distracted by other people's less-than-unicorn-worthy behavior and instead going full unicorn yourself, even when you'd rather go the way of the snake, can help you to feel good about what you do, as well as make it easier to get the job done.

In the work world, there are two kinds of people: those who make the most of it and those who make the worst of it. Ironically, the latter are actually making jobs they hate even harder for themselves (and probably their coworkers). We've all heard that it takes more muscles to frown than to smile. Even if that isn't true literally, it certainly is figuratively. It reminds me of when I was a kid and my parents would take me to some museum or fort or another place I did not want to go. I would drag ten paces behind, stomping and grumbling and crinkling up my face.

"You can spend the day being all grumpy, and the rest of us will happily ignore you. Or you can act like you're having fun and, before you know it, you just might be," Daddy would say to me. I hated to admit it, but he was right. I would find something about the place I liked—buttons to press or photos of bank robbers or whatever. I would throw myself in, and, before I knew it, I was in the gift shop, eating ice cream and saying, "That was kind of fun."

I've done the same thing with several jobs I've had that
I really didn't care for. Some days, doing that feels more
natural than others. Some jobs make it next to impossible.
But I know that adding to the problem with my own crummy
attitude really doesn't make things worse for anyone but me.
Admitting that is the worst. Sometimes I want to complain
and stomp and grumble and be altogether unpleasant to be
around. But you know what? It makes people not want to be
around me. Go figure. And the only thing worse than doing a
tedious job you don't like is having to do it alone.

Being That Unicorn can also make it easier to land a job. My
dad says I've never gotten a job for which I'm qualified, so
I suppose I've always been a unicorn. I figure, with a little
magic, I'll be able to figure it out. And so far, so good. A
unicorn says, "Yes." A unicorn says, "I can do that." And then
a unicorn figures it out. Sure, this won't work for being a
brain surgeon or a commercial pilot. But there are a plethora
of jobs for which it will work. And if you already are a brain
surgeon or a commercial pilot, it can certainly get you to the
next level in your career...whatever that might be!

Unicorns also have a tendency to reinvent themselves.
I've been an actress, a law student, a production assistant,
a college professor, an artist's model, a dance teacher,
a camp activities director, a speaker, and, of course, an
author and writer. I wanted to do all of those things. I knew
deep down that I could do all of those things. So I used my

skills at one job to help me to get a position in another. If you look hard enough, almost every job shares a certain number of skills with others, including positions that aren't particularly similar.

Working takes work. There's no getting around that. Just like with everything else, the only things we can change are ourselves, our attitudes, and our reactions. So you have to ask yourself, "What's it going to be?" If your answer is the way of the unicorn, you're already on the right track.

When it comes to working, That Unicorn acknowledges that...

Work is called work for a reason.

Work can be downright tedious. Generally, you won't like all of the people you're working with. Even That Unicorn has to be okay with that, because that's just how it is. Sure, you may have a dream scenario where you love your work, you love your coworkers, and you love Mondays. Good for you. But if you don't, that's okay, too.

Most of us have to work in some capacity—some of us inside the home, others outside. Some of us work for ourselves, others for companies or individuals. Some of us work for traditional salaries, others for trade or as volunteers. Nearly everyone does some kind of work, and almost all of that work has some sort of downside. But downsides can be good for us. I'm not talking about having to deal with inhumane conditions or impossible bosses. I'm talking about learning to deal with the challenges that work presents.

If we only did whatever we wanted, whenever we wanted, wherever we wanted, it would be tough for us to become productive people who are able to function within a society of other people. Remember those rich kids who were breaking into the homes of celebrities and stealing from them? That's the definition of not learning the value of hard work. It may sound old-fashioned, even cliché. But That Unicorn knows how good it feels to work at something that is difficult and succeed. There's nothing like it in the world.

It still counts even if you get help.

I'm not sure where the myth of "you have to do it alone, or you didn't really do it" came from, but I do know that it's ridiculous. Sometimes you can't get help. That's one thing, and, when a unicorn has to be an island, That Unicorn can and will. But that is very rare, considering the virtual access—let alone the real access—we have to all sorts of help when it comes to all kinds of things.

I get the thought process: "This is my job. I'm supposed to know how to do it. If I can't get it done, what's wrong with me?" But that is flawed thinking. And it is most certainly not unicorn thinking. That Unicorn knows that jobs come with some parts that are more difficult than others, and, even if we're really good at our job, we may still encounter a roadblock now and then. It's not a matter of whether or not you will come up against challenges. The real question is: how will you handle those challenges?

That Unicorn knows there is always someone to call or email. There is always research to be done. There is always an answer. Even if the solution is not in our heads, the way to get that solution is to seek help. The smartest, most successful people are those who know who and when to ask how to get the job done, whatever that job may be.

Impostor syndrome is a real thing.

It's a fascinating phenomenon. Here we are, finally, a college student or a mom or a PhD candidate or a speaker at a conference or a CEO, and, all of a sudden, we wonder, "How did I get here? And when is someone going to figure out that I don't belong here?" We figure the thing we're doing is too amazing for us to be doing it.

Rest assured, you're not alone in that feeling, and there's nothing wrong with it; this too shall pass. When it comes, That Unicorn knows to replace it with gratitude. Your mind says, "I feel like I don't deserve this, that I'm not really an expert, that what I say or do shouldn't really matter. The reason I feel those things is that I actually feel so incredibly lucky for the fact that I do deserve it, that I am an expert, and that what I say and do does matter, that I simply can't quite believe it. So, instead of questioning it, I will give thanks for it."

That is the way of the unicorn. To accept the uneasy feeling, to thank it for reminding of us how amazing it is that we get to be exactly where we are, and then letting it go so that we can go on being our fabulous unicorn selves.

Not every unicorn gets her dream job.

If you're thinking that you can't be That Unicorn unless you get *that* job, think again...especially if the job you want is actress or rock star or astronaut or another type of one-in-a-million gig. Unicorns know that there are so many things at which they can shine. The goal is to find the one that really belongs to you or that you can bring your own magic to, despite its less-than-shiny looks.

Sometimes, That Unicorn will end up working in a less-than-ideal gig. If that's the case, then they'll be the best at whatever that thing is. People used to ask me how I could be so chipper as I hit hour seven of delivering beer to football-watching guys who thought the temperature of their beer was the most crucial thing in the universe. The truth was, sometimes I wanted to pour those beers over their heads. But, most of the time, it made the job more fun if I made stupid jokes and smiled and sang along with the bad '80s music playing over the worn-out bar speakers. It was my choice to make the best or the worst of the situation.

Unicorns know that our jobs don't define us. It's how we choose to do that job that defines us. I'm not suggesting this is always easy or possible. I've cried on the job, wished for a natural disaster, and behaved in ways that I am not proud of. But being That Unicorn is not about anything more than doing your best at that moment. And (there's no way around it) that is easier at some times than at others.

Money isn't the measure of a job's importance.

We live in a world where money rules the roost in many ways. It's all about who you're wearing, what you're driving, and whether not you can see it and like it and want it and buy it. Even though there is a tremendous value placed on how much money one has, not every important or rewarding job will be a high-paying one.

That Unicorn uses paychecks for the purchase of things, not for the valuing of life. Lots of very unimportant jobs pay lots of money, like throwing the stuffed skin of a pig from one end of a lawn to another or being a human clothes hanger so that other people can make money from the fact that you make those clothes look so good. And lots of incredibly important jobs, like educating the very people who will run the world one day or doing all the dirty work that doctors don't, get paid relatively little. It simply doesn't make any sense.

Seeing her own worth and ignoring the judgment of others is one of That Unicorn's most exceptional skills. Unicorns know who they are and what they do and what is important in the world. They find the value in their work and do it to the best of their abilities. Period.

Volunteer work is work.

Volunteer work is so important and yet all too often undervalued. That's a shift that unicorns can help to make. That Unicorn recognizes that volunteering qualifies as work and appreciates the contributions that others make as well. It seems so odd that helping others would be undervalued. But just try telling people that you don't earn money but rather spend your time volunteering, and half of them will think you're some sort of kept spouse and the other half will think you're living off handouts of one kind or another.

That Unicorn knows that volunteering is not only work but vital work, work that keeps the world moving forward. I don't do enough of it, and I always say I will do more. It is one of the things on my BTU Evolution List. The more we volunteer, the more we come to appreciate both those who have less than we do and how much we can accomplish by giving our time.

I don't know if it's true because it's cheesy or it's cheesy because it's true. But I do know that when we give of ourselves, we get closer to being our very best selves. I'm not even sure we can ultimately be our best selves—or That Unicorn for that matter—without offering our time for the sake of others. If you think about it, it just might be the shortest path to our best world.

Unicorns lose it at work.

Sometimes unicorns lose their cool. They say more than they meant to say to the wrong person. They storm out of meetings. They raise their voices. They conduct themselves in less-than-unicorn-like ways. It happens. What unicorns don't do is turn in their horns because of it.

We want to always be our best selves, to take things in stride, to learn from our mistakes, to be humble. But work is one place that really challenges even the most evolved of unicorns. So many personalities and stressors. So many things that are simply out of our control. It's no wonder that sometimes our less-than-best selves rear their ugly heads.

We can't control other people, ever. And we certainly can't control systems and policies and technology. And, every now and then, we can't even control our own reactions to their working less than optimally. What we always have control over is how we regroup after that behavior.

Teamwork is only as good as the sum of its members.

If you have the chance, pick your team members. If you can't pick them, have a hand in assigning who does what. Groups are tough. On the one hand, working with others is the best way to get a job done—more heads are better than one and all that. On the other hand, if there are members who don't want to participate or who aren't skilled at what needs to be done, it can create even more work. You may have to chase after them, at best, or fix or do their work entirely, at worst.

Teams work when every member on the team works. When That Unicorn is put in a team situation, she does her best to get the right people in the right tasks, whether by leading the group or simply playing a part in getting the right person to take the lead.

If all else fails, That Unicorn focuses on the work at hand, and on documenting, documenting, documenting. If the group goes off the rails, it's vital to be able to show where things went awry. That Unicorn knows that it's never kind to throw someone under the bus and that there is also nothing wrong with self-protection. The unicorn code is built on fairness, honesty, and transparency.

Unicorns learn on the job.

You don't have to know it all to apply for or accept a job. That Unicorn would never lie on a résumé or at a job interview. But there's nothing wrong with noting how your experience can translate to the new gig even if you'll need to learn as you go.

That's one of the greatest unicorn strengths, being able to run in and pick up the skills needed for the work at hand all along the way. It's actually what keeps things fun and engaging for That Unicorn. Don't be afraid of messing up. Too many people avoid doing things because they are worried they won't do them perfectly right out of the gate. Forget that—get your hands dirty. You will get it right in the end because you are That Unicorn.

The only one who expects perfection on the first day is you. So let that stuff go. Everyone has had a first day of school, a first day on the job, a first at something where they wanted to do their best but didn't even know how just yet. If you wait until you know it all, you'll never do anything, because—news flash—not even the unicorn with the sparkliest, flowiest mane knows it all.

10 Do what you know is right without expectation of rewards or praise.

I like to exceed expectations. I like to push myself and surprise the person for whom I am working. But I do it only for me, knowing I will likely never get a bonus or raise or even an "attagirl." I dig it. So I do it. If a reward comes, awesome. That's gravy. But unicorns only exceed expectations because they like how it makes them feel.

Now, when it comes to kindness and generosity, I believe that we should always exceed expectations. You don't have to call the customer service agent by name and ask how her day was. But you should. You don't have to tell the janitor how much you appreciate how great your office looks every morning. But you should. You don't have to hold the elevator or wipe up the spill or say "*Gesundheit*" when someone sneezes. But, yes, you should.

Unicorns wants to be their best selves and live their best lives, and they want the same for everyone around them. Deep down, they also want to heal the world. If everyone exceeded expectations, in the workplace and away from it, the world would be nothing but ribbons and rainbows and herds of one-horned creatures with manes glittering in the wind. Until then, exceed the kindness quotient and hope for a mass contagion of all that is right and good...

CHAPTER FOUR

———

How to BTU when **Playing**

Playing should be fun. Unfortunately, it isn't always. Why?
Because we are too much in our heads or because others
are making it hard for us. If we are too busy trying to "do it
right," it's next to impossible to enjoy. And if someone else
is obsessed with perfection, that can sap the joy from any
activity as well. But a unicorn knows how to play. Unicorns
know how to kick up their heels. They allow themselves—and
everyone around them—to revel in the joy.

Playing is easy when you're a kid. You don't think about
it, you just do it. Even in the face of so much technology,
kids still make spaceships out of boxes and pretend they're
cowboys and dance around like rock stars and act silly for no
reason other than that it feels good. But, eventually, playing
gives way to competition, and either you're first-string or
stuck on the bench or made to do something you're lousy
at and given a trophy in the name of not hurting your self-
esteem. Can you say "backfire?"

Even if it's just a board game or a family game of tag football
or charades with friends, it can be very hard to really play
when you are too busy managing a gaggle of personalities—
including your own—which may be inclined to the "win or
die" or "take no prisoners" attitude that has ruined more than
one Monopoly session in my house.

Here's what I know. People need to play, and they need to
compete. Cheating hurts everyone. Not everyone can be a

winner every time. Losing is okay, too. And we've gotten too damn serious about everything. That Unicorn knows how to have fun, but not at the expense of others. She knows how to make a fool of herself, even in a packed theater as she puts on as many pairs of SpongeBob SquarePants undies as possible in pursuit of winning the "privilege" of being slimed.

Yes, that was me. Yes, we won. Yes, we got slimed. And, yes, my daughter could not have been any more thrilled. And I would have missed it all if I had been too embarrassed to play or too afraid to lose or too obsessed with winning. We just played. That Unicorn knows how to (and loves to) just play.

Whether it's playing for playing's sake or competing in some sort of game or sport, being That Unicorn is always the best strategy. You don't have to be better than anyone. You don't have to make excuses for not being the best. You don't have to tear down the people who are good at the thing. You don't have to win. You don't have to worry about losing. It's acceptable to fall or fail or mess up. The goal of playing is to play.

When it comes to playing, That Unicorn acknowledges that...

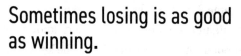

Sometimes losing is as good as winning.

I get that that might sound crazy to some people. How on earth could the high of winning, of validating your prowess, of beating out someone else for the top spot be outshone by losing? We don't give losing enough credit. Losing reminds us that sometimes people lose and allows us to be empathetic when someone else does. If we don't get the chance to stand in other people's shoes, we can't ever truly understand what they are feeling. When we lose, we can later be a shoulder for someone else to cry on when they lose.

That Unicorn knows that there is something great about losing, about feeling that zap, that zing, that reminder that we need to train harder or study more or play more often. If we always win, it can lead to a boredom of sorts as well as a swollen head: the former of which is no good to us, the latter of which is no good to others. I think Tiger Woods suffered from never losing: when you think you're invincible and nothing is ever good enough, you cheat on your supermodel wife and are shocked when you get caught, and are even more shocked when there are consequences for your actions.

When we lose, we also have the chance to celebrate the winner. That Unicorn knows how to enjoy the glow of someone else's win. Unicorns are so at ease with themselves that they have nothing to prove. They're good with who they are, whether they win or lose, which means they can be happy for someone else's win. When you win some and you lose some, you can revel in the victories and learn from the losses without ever feeling like a failure.

When you play the game, whatever that game might be and whether it be literal or figurative, you may lose or you may win. Regardless, That Unicorn will always learn.

Sometimes you're going to lose.

It's okay to want to win every time, as long as you're also okay with losing. There's nothing wrong with wanting to win. It would be tough to step up to the plate or sit down to the table or walk up to the tee if you possessed no drive to win. The spirit of competition can be healthy. But only if you are as okay with losing as you are with winning. I'm not suggesting that you need to be wishy-washy. But if you're going to play, you have to know that winning is not the only possibility.

If, every time you lose, you go into a spiraling slump or storm out of the game or are unkind to the winner or the other players, you're not just a bad sport, you're also not a unicorn. (And, if we're being honest, you're not a very nice person, either.) Sure, you can be bummed, especially if you lost money or another type of prize or accolades for which you were hoping. But you simply cannot assume you are always going to win and decompensate when you lose. That simply does not suit That Unicorn.

For one thing, when you do win, it will make it very hard for others to celebrate you and your win when they know how awful you were when you didn't win. Playing is about the game. If it's only about the success, then you're missing the point. That Unicorn is as good a winner as a loser, equally gracious and always ready for the next game.

 ## Games are supposed to be fun.

When they stop being fun, stop playing. If you find yourself resenting taking part in whatever you're playing, it's time to find a new game. If you are focused solely on grinding your partner into the dirt, it's time to take a step back and look at what your true intentions are. Are you here to play, or are you here to settle a wholly different score?

That can be a tough question to ask and to answer, which is part of why it is such an important question. Have you chosen a particular game because you know you can win? Is the only reason you opted to play that you want to beat your opponent at something? Is there a conversation that is really needed, but you want to tangle with your feelings in a less direct way?

If any of those answers is yes, you're not playing for fun. You're playing for resolution.

There is little chance that the answers or resolutions you're seeking will come from tackling things in such a roundabout way. So don't ruin things for yourself or for the others involved. Don't play if the purpose is not playing. They are called games for a reason. And we don't have to be talking about literal games, either—we can be talking about any leisure activity. Don't do it unless you enjoy it.

Helping someone else can feel even better than winning.

That may seem hard to believe at first glance, but it's true. Helping someone else and then basking in the glow of their giddiness at winning feels really, really good. It sometimes feels even better than enjoying your own win, because you don't also have to feel like you caused someone else to feel sad.

Think about all those times you've seen runners stop to help someone who has fallen or hold someone up so they can finish together. The point of play is pleasure. It's not about confirming that you're the best one. Truly.

Sportsmanship, working together, and thinking about the other people with whom you are playing or competing gives so much depth to a playful experience. Even if you won't get to the top of the rock until a week later, you can only ski the blue and not the black, or if you only catch three fish instead of ten, being able to enjoy that experience with someone else or enjoy someone else's success in that experience can be so much more rewarding and give real value to our play time.

No one likes a sore winner.

When you do win, there's no reason to make everyone else feel like a loser; the only thing worse than a sore loser is a sore winner. Rubbing it in is not very unicorn-like. Bragging and carrying on is no fun for the others with whom you are playing. And you can bet that no one will want to play with you again if you act that way.

That Unicorn just wouldn't act that way. It's beneath That Unicorn, honestly. Making others feel bad about not winning doesn't serve any purpose. I get it. It can be tough to resist when you play with people who continuously talk about how great they are at this or that and who "shit-talk" throughout the game. But I have a little secret to tell you: not bragging actually burns people like that even more.

Unkind people like to bring others down to their level. Trolls love to drag unicorns down into the mud. Don't let them. Toss your mane, offer your hand and a sincere "Good game," and move along. You already won.

No one likes a sore loser, either.

If you lose, don't make the winner feel like winning wasn't worth it (even if your opponent isn't being very unicorn-like). Don't falsely accuse the winner of cheating. Don't make a bunch of excuses for why you lost and they won. It is unlikely that a unicorn would exhibit such unseemly behavior. It can be tempting when the game was close or if the winner is a sore one or, heck, even if you've just had a bad day or a bad run.

But this isn't the place for it. That Unicorn knows that the winner has a right to enjoy winning. Playing isn't just about winning. But winning is fun, or can be anyway. If you make the winner feel lousy, they won't want to play again. And it might not just be this game that they don't want to join you in. Bad losing behavior just may sour your relationship in a much grander way as well.

It would be truly a shame to tarnish a friendship or mess up a marriage or lose a relative over your behavior at play. If you can't handle both possible outcomes, you have no business playing in the first place.

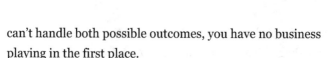

Unicorns don't cheat.

We just don't. That really takes the fun out of things. We don't swipe an extra card or move a tile when no one's looking or add additional points to our tally. Cheating is way worse than losing. That Unicorn knows that there's no joy in deception.

If you feel compelled to cheat, you have to ask yourself why. If it's because the people with whom you're playing are unkind when you lose, don't play with them anymore. If it's because you wish you were better at the game or the sport or the activity, take lessons or practice or do whatever you need to do to get better. If it's because you need to win to feel good about yourself, you need to polish your horn and comb your mane—unicorns don't need to win to feel good about themselves, they just need to know they did their best.

There's no good reason for cheating. We learn when we play— we learn about ourselves, about the activity we're engaged in, and about the people with whom we are playing. If we cheat, we don't learn anything because we're too focused on manipulating a win. That Unicorn doesn't cheat. That Unicorn would always much rather lose gracefully.

Unicorns don't stand by while others cheat.

It's no fun being put in the position of knowing that others are cheating. Unicorns have a zero-tolerance policy when it comes to cheating, which means that That Unicorn has two choices: excuse herself from the play or call it out—nicely, of course. Neither of those choices is particularly easy. But being That Unicorn isn't about taking the easy way out.

You always have the right to say, "I'm done playing." The thing is, you may be asked why, which may mean calling out the cheating anyway, or lying. I don't generally condone lying. But if a white lie would save the situation, I would never blame a unicorn for opting for that route. When might that be called for? Well, if the person who's cheating is going to handle being called out poorly at best and atrociously at worst.

If you can't—or don't want to—address the cheating at the moment, you can always excuse yourself and talk to the person later. Or change things up in the moment to make it impossible—or at least harder—for that person to cheat. "Okay. I'm going to play banker for the rest of the game." Or, "I'm going to take over keeping score. I need the practice." Or, "How about we all dump our tiles and pick again?" You can look at the cheater knowingly and hope the message will be received without any drama. That Unicorn doesn't support cheating because cheating hurts everyone.

It's no fun if everyone gets a trophy.

Even if being okay with losing or winning is key to being That Unicorn, that doesn't mean everyone is a winner. Why? Because, if play fails to recognize that we are all good at something but some of us are better at some things than others, we are denying the power of being recognized for our talents.

If everyone gets a ribbon, than the meaning of that ribbon is zilch. Sometimes playing is only about playing. But playing can also be about improving our skills. Skill improvement certainly is a reward unto itself, but so are trophies and accolades. I think it's sad that we don't celebrate someone when they are outstanding at something. Medals shouldn't just be for the Olympics, but they should be only for those who excel at their game.

I'm not sure when we started giving everyone a trophy for participation, but it waters things down and, honestly, makes me feel silly. I don't want a medal for participating. I participated because I wanted to. To be pandered to, like "Look at you! You participated!" makes it seem as if I cannot

be trusted with being self-aware. I didn't win at sports as
a kid. But I did get the lead roles in plays and musicals.
I learned to honor my talents and to honor the talents of
others. That Unicorn is able to celebrate the achievements
of others without needing a pat on her own head for merely
showing up.

10 Competition is good for unicorns.

Whether we are competing against ourselves
or others, being competitive is about pushing ourselves to
try harder, to go faster, to practice longer. Without it, it
can be too easy to rest on our laurels. That doesn't mean
everything should be a competition. In fact, there should be
plenty of play in your life in which there isn't even a winner
to be named.

But there should also be challenge in our lives. That Unicorn
commits to being her best self. And being one's best self
requires some pushing—sometimes externally, sometimes
internally, sometimes a little of both. Competition is that
push. It's that voice that says, "You can do it! Keep going!"
And hearing that voice, well, it feels good, especially when
it's right.

And when that voice is wrong, when we can't do one more or go any further or think of the answer, we are humbled in that moment and are hopefully reminded that not everyone is good at everything. However, everyone is good at something, and that's what's so great about life and all the play it allows us. And, hopefully, it compels us to get back up and try it again or even to find a new game. The important thing is that we have enough competition in our lives to drive us. You may need very little, while others might need a ton. That Unicorn seeks the balance that works best in her life.

CHAPTER FIVE

———

How to BTU When **Dating**

Dating can be tough. But being That Unicorn can make it much more manageable. Trust me. Dating is about three unicorn pillars: trusting yourself, trusting the process, and trusting others. Any one of those things can be tricky on its own. But trying to do all three at once can be a veritable Cirque du Soleil-level juggling act. Looking for love? It's an ideal time to summon your inner unicorn.

For starters, it can be hard to know where to look, and where not to look, for that matter. It's always best to start with friends of friends—that helps you vet the person with whom you're thinking about sharing your heart. Matchmakers can work but can be pricey. These days, dating apps are probably the most popular means. But do your homework online, and trust your inner unicorn. If something doesn't seem right, steer clear, and only meet in public places with lots of other people around until you are confident that who you're talking to is the real deal and that you're safe.

That Unicorn knows that, when it comes to dating, there's no rush. Take your time. The world, much like car dealerships, would have you think there's some kind of rush, as if there won't be the same lot full of cars tomorrow. Your match isn't going anywhere. Your person is looking for you, too. If you rush things, if you push things, if you ignore your inner unicorn, I can almost guarantee you won't end up in the best relationship with the best person.

As you look for your match, keep in mind that the only person you can change is you. Sure, you might be able to suggest a haircut or better-fitting jeans, or help someone feel confident enough to apply for that promotion or try that new spin class. But ultimately, who you meet is who you're getting. Trust me, starting out a relationship with the attitude that you can simply change what doesn't suit you is a non-starter.

If they don't earn what you think they should, you can change your expectations. If they don't look like who you thought you'd be with, you can change your thinking. If they just are not your cup of tea, you can change your idea of who "the one" is, or you can move on. Don't count on altering who she or he is. That is guaranteed to end in disappointment, likely for both of you.

So how do you know when you've found the one? That's the million-dollar question. The answer is the worst. So, brace yourself. When you know, you know. Big help, right? This is one of those times when you have to really trust that you are That Unicorn and you know what's best for you. Do you believe this person? Do you have faith in this person? Do you enjoy this person? Can you imagine caring for this person as they age or if they fall ill? Can you imagine they will care for you? Do you feel safe and loved and desired? Do they get you? You'll know. You just have to trust me on this one. You'll know.

When it comes to dating, That Unicorn acknowledges that...

You must trust your inner unicorn.

This is a hard one. Believe me, I know. The thing is, most of us think we know how to listen to and trust the voice inside us. But too many of us actually don't. Humans are stubborn. We hear what we want to hear. But if we take the time to quiet our minds and really listen, we will know which trails to follow and which to leave cold.

Each of our inner unicorns possesses a sacred knowledge about who we really are and what we truly need. We may not be totally aligned with that knowledge, because it goes against what the world says we should want, what our parents or friends want for us, or what our religion or culture attempts to dictate. That is the noise that can make it hard for our inner unicorn to make itself heard.

The trick is to think about the source of our feelings. Why do we want someone tall or young or short or old? Why do we want someone from one place or another? Why is this trait more critical than that one? What you will find is that, if you peel away all those perceived desires, realizing that they come from nothing more than rom-coms and overbearing relatives and outdated religious beliefs, you can truly understand what you actually want. You can find someone to date who truly brings contentment to your inner unicorn who, ultimately, always knows best.

"The one" may surprise you.

It's okay for the one you choose to be totally different from who you *thought* you'd choose. In fact, it's more than okay—it's probably excellent news. Why? Because it means you were able to draw back the curtains of nonsense that were composed of all the messaging around you and were ultimately able to see the reality of who you should be looking for when it comes to finding "the one."

It's also vital to note that there likely isn't really a "one." It's more likely there are "the ones"—a variety of people who could be a good fit for you. That's what dating really should be about. It shouldn't be about kissing a bunch of frogs. It should be about adventuring with a variety of princes and/or princesses. Dating is not about finding someone to change. Dating is not about lining up all the usual suspects prescribed by a world that doesn't really know you, let alone the real you. Dating is not about throwing caution to the wind and hoping for the best.

Dating is about listening. It's about listening to yourself and to the people who show interest in you. Do you really want a person who (fill-in-the-blank), or is that just something you've been made to think you want? If you love pizza, but you think you "should" be with someone with a more sophisticated palate, how long do you think it will be before you start resenting the fact that a gooey pie of joy hasn't graced your table in eons? It's an oversimplification, but it's true. If you date people who suit an imaginary you, the real you doesn't stand a chance of ever finding happiness.

A unicorn can always change her mind.

In the opera, they say, "It's not over until the fat lady sings." In dating, we generally say, "It's not over until there's a ring." But the truth is, it doesn't matter how many divas have sung their arias or how many diamonds have encircled one's finger—it's not over until you say so. A unicorn always has the right to change her mind. After one date, after a hundred, even after an engagement. The truth is, even marriage isn't the end of the line. (More on that later.)

There is something incredibly empowering about remembering that dating is in no way a forced march. You don't have to do it at all, for one. You don't have to do it any specific way, as long as you and your dating prospects are in agreement. You can change your course at any time. Online dating not working? You can shut down all your accounts

and try speed-dating instead. Friends keep setting you up
to no avail? You can tell them enough is enough. Hired a
matchmaker who's been more like a mis-matchmaker? Fire
her. Maybe you should try going out with that lawyer your
mom can't stop talking about...

Dating is about you first. It's about *you* finding what works
for *you*. *Then* it's about who you're dating. This is a time
when you have to put you first. Be kind. Be respectful. Don't
ghost people. But don't go out with someone again because
you don't want to hurt their feelings or someone else's—like
the mutual friend or colleague you share or who set you up.
That never leads to anywhere good. If things aren't working,
say so. Dating is like shopping. If it doesn't fit, there's no need
to keep trying it on, and there is *definitely* no reason to buy it.
You think returns are hard at the store? Try divorce court.

Dating knows no timeline.

This is the good news and the bad news. The good
news is that there's no clock ticking, no matter what
your friends (and popular culture) say. That Unicorn knows
that finding the one takes as long as it takes. There's no need
for self-flagellation because "it's taking forever." You might
not know after one date or ten if you're ready to commit
to forever. And you don't have to see each other every day

or even every weekend. You can only date in whatever way works for you and the people you are dating.

Now for the bad news. Since there is no timeline, dating can feel amorphous and like the process is dragging on forever. It can feel unsettling not to have a deadline of sorts. By this point, we should have been on this many dates or should feel this way or should be closer to knowing if this person is indeed "the one." But, no matter how you cut it, there is no such timeline to dating, and anyone who tells you otherwise is selling you a false bill of goods. It may make you feel better in the moment to think there are some sort of rules or some kind of timeline. That sort of boundary can be comforting. But it's only an illusion.

There is no timeline when it comes to dating, barring the one that you and the other person develop as you go along. There's nothing wrong with checking in with each other and talking about it. But there's no real use in setting arbitrary deadlines that may or may not match up with what your inner unicorn is telling you.

People find partners.

The process works...but only if you trust it. Dating does work; people do find partners. Some even find their very own versions of happily ever after. Making it work for you is a two-fold process. One, you have to accept that the expression "the process" is a bit of a misnomer. Second, you have to trust it without exception.

Calling it "the process" is misleading because dating isn't one single process in any sense. There are so many ways to date, and the only wrong way is the one that doesn't work for you. It's great to read about dating and talk to friends and family about what works for them. But it doesn't do any good to get too attached to one way of doing things. "The Rules" only work for the people for whom they work. I know. I know. It would be so much nicer if there were a tidy path all laid out and following it led to a life of love filled with ribbons and roses and rabbits hopping through a fairy-tale field. Sorry. The only real unicorn—is you.

Trust is the number-one most crucial element when it comes to dating. And one of the things you have to trust blindly is that dating works. Not every kind of dating works for every type of person. But dating of some sort works for nearly every kind of person. You can't find your someone unless you engage with at least a couple of someones. Partners rarely fall out of the sky. Falling in love is almost always preceded by dating. It's just the way it goes. Trust me...and trust it.

New doesn't equal bad.

Just because a process is new to you doesn't mean it's not worth a try.

Dating has morphed and changed over the years and through every generation. There are some tried-and-true methods that continue to work for some. But there are also new and inventive ways to date popping up all the time. To ignore those is to limit your chances of finding the very thing for which you are looking.

It doesn't make sense to ignore what is new simply because it is new. I get it. You see a new way to meet people or to date, and you think, "Great—just what I need. Another app or event or scheme to throw my time and money at and still end up no better off than I was before." But imagine if we had thought that about cars or phones or the internet. Sure, it makes sense to have a reasonable amount of distrust in the beginning and tempered expectations about what the new thing can do for you. But you have to give things a try.

Though often credited to Albert Einstein, it was Rita Mae Brown who wrote in a novel, "Insanity is doing the same thing over and over again, but expecting different results." It's not surprising that a lesser-known female genius wrote that and a well-known male genius had it attributed to him. Still, it couldn't be any more true, especially when it comes to dating. If you date in the same way over and over, expecting things to somehow suddenly go differently simply doesn't make sense. You have to change things up, and you have to trust the people in the know to know what new methods just might lead you down the path to happily ever after.

You're an "other" to someone else.

You can be trusted. One of the hardest things in the world can be trusting other people, especially when we've been hurt or duped, or worse, in the past. One way to help to learn to trust others is to remember that you are an "other" to people who don't know you. Your friends are "others." Your family members are "others." People you know and love are "others" to people who don't know and love them. You and your family and friends are good people. That means there have to be at least some other good people out there who you don't know.

Keeping in mind your own otherness can help you to truly be That Unicorn by honoring the fact that, just as you are suspicious of that other person, they are cautious about you, too. You have to be. The world is a big, wild place. It is also a wonderful place. When we look at the world from that perspective, we are being That Unicorn. We are opening ourselves up to discovering who we can trust while remaining vigilant and smart.

You can be trusted, which means there are other people out there who can be trusted, too. That doesn't mean going home, getting into a car, or going somewhere isolated with someone you don't know. But it does mean that you have to trust new people enough to grab a cup of coffee in public during the day and then take cautious steps from there as you build trust between the two of you. Trusting people can be the hardest thing in the world. It can also be the most rewarding.

Your inner unicorn knows who you can trust.

Follow your instincts. Do not ignore red flags, not even the teeny ones barely blowing in the breeze. All too often, we ignore the signs. We tell our gut to relax. We ignore our inner unicorn because we want so badly for this one to be the one. But this is a top unicorn no-no. If your mane is bristling, walk away.

You know that expression about trying to make a square peg fit into a round hole? That's similar to what ignoring your instincts about someone feels like. They keep doing things that set off alarm bells for you, but you explain them away. And the more alarm bells get set off, the more explaining away you do. The signals get louder, the explanations get wilder, and, one way or another, things go badly.

That Unicorn always trusts her inner unicorn. It's not always fun to have to listen to that inner voice. It can be downright disappointing and feel terribly dull. But if things seem too good to be true, seem off in a way that you can't quite put your finger on, or if you find yourself crafting elaborate tales to quell your friends' fears, let alone your own, it's time to let this one off the line and fish in another stream.

You have to believe people's actions.

People's actions reveal their truth. If someone shows themself to be trustworthy, then trust them. If they do things that clearly delineate untrustworthiness, heed that as well. People will say all sorts of things to get what they want and to fool people into believing they are something or someone they are not. But their actions will often contradict their words. And it is always actions above words that you should believe.

This is another instance where wanting to believe something can override our knowing that something simply is not true. But That Unicorn knows it is better to take heed of someone's actions the first time than to end up sorry later. "When someone shows you who they are, believe them the first time," Maya Angelou once said. Her words are what unicorn mottoes are made of—hard truths that serve us well.

Dating is tricky. You want to be hopeful and optimistic and open. But, at the same time, you need to be cautious and realistic and protective of yourself as well. That Unicorn knows just how to strike that balance, and trusting who people show you they are plays a huge part in that. Anyone can say words. That Unicorn only wants a partner who can walk the walk right alongside her. Settling for anything less would be just that, settling.

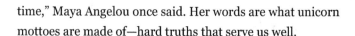

Trusting the universe is essential.

Ultimately, whether we're talking about dating or anything else, you have to come to a place where you simply trust the universe. Not blindly. Not foolishly. Not with wild abandon. But with eyes open and brain engaged and heart and soul focused on what you know is real.

The magic of That Unicorn lies in knowing that the universe can be trusted. Sometimes, even That Unicorn falters when it comes to trusting the universe, especially after a particularly bad date or a weekend with no swipes in the right direction or a set-up looming that you can already tell won't work. It's wild, but the universe knows. It has our backs. It's rarely a straight line, and it's virtually never precisely what we expect. But, somehow, it generally gets us there.

We can be our very own worst enemy when it comes to dating (or to a lot of things, for that matter). We fight stuff because we can't believe it could be true. My wife and I met on Tinder. Her friends all told her I wasn't real, that I was catfishing her. But she says that, despite their protests, she knew there was a real girl behind those texts, and she really looked like her photos (in good lighting anyway). She says the universe told her it was time. She could feel it in her bones. She knew she could trust what she was feeling. You have to learn to trust what you're feeling, too.

CHAPTER SIX

How to BTU When **Loving**

Loving someone is the easiest—and the hardest—thing to do. To love someone truly, freely, and honestly is heavenly...until it isn't. And even if it *is* true love, it certainly is not always going to be divine. But when you let your inner unicorn take over, it can be a heck of a lot easier. Enjoying a happy, loving relationship depends on several things. Two of the most important things are 1) that your partner loves you, and 2) that your partner is different from you.

Much of this applies to being a parent, a friend, a sibling, a son, or a daughter as well. Whether it's your romantic partner or anyone else, love requires patience and kindness and honesty. We're bombarded with messaging that suggests that loving someone—regardless of the relationship—is somehow the easiest thing in the world to do. But while feeling love is easy, showing it is another matter altogether.

For example, it's not always a cakewalk for parents to love their children. Sometimes they do things that make you want to scream. That Unicorn freely admits that because That Unicorn knows the importance of eliminating every possible kind of stigma. Hiding how hard something is doesn't help anyone, and that couldn't be any more true when it comes to love. As long as we walk around wishing for something that doesn't exist, we'll always think that we have somehow failed, that we must not really be That Unicorn—otherwise love would be easy and our relationships would look like they do in the movies.

In too many ways, when it comes to romantic love, it feels like it's supposed to be completely carefree. It's supposed to be sentimental dates and shared whispers and eternal desire. Hopefully, that will be a massive part of it...but just a part. Real love is about committing to someone and all the elements that make up who that someone is.

Real love is knowing how important that ugly vase is to your partner and putting her coffee cup in the dishwasher every morning and listening to how stressful work is and letting her backseat-drive when you bring her home from the hospital. Love is knowing that the depth to which she loves you is worth all of it, even the casserole she insists on making for every family event that no one eats except her. It's not being with someone "in spite of;" it is genuinely loving someone "because of"...including the habits that make you crazy, because plenty of habits about you drive your partner crazy, too.

That Unicorn loves fully and openly. She's smart enough to protect her heart, but also willing to let others in even though she knows she may get hurt. When you give that kind of love, that's precisely the kind of love you can expect to get back. The most important thing you can do on this path is to always allow your inner unicorn to be your guide.

When it comes to loving, That Unicorn acknowledges that...

Love and abundance are always the foundation.

That Unicorn always operates from a place of love and abundance, rather than fear and scarcity. I don't always operate from a place of love and abundance—I want to, but I don't. The thing is, that's okay as long as I recognize and recalibrate when I get off course. That Unicorn is a conscious creature who checks in with herself about how she's acting and why.

Operating from a place of love and abundance means we are making choices and behaving in a way that is loving to ourselves and to our partners. It means knowing that there is plenty of love to give and receive. There is no place for being stingy with our affections. When we are, we have to stop and ask ourselves why. Generally, it's because we are not feeling abundantly loved.

But if we withhold, all we are doing is perpetuating an unhappy cycle. That Unicorn takes a breath and reminds herself, "I am loved. I have plenty of love to give. And I am fully open to receiving the love being offered to me." For anyone who has been abused or hurt, it can be hard to operate consistently from this place, because we have learned to protect ourselves. We've built ourselves a cozy little cell. But, as safe as it may feel, it is equally cold. That Unicorn is continually working on forgiving the past and relishing the present.

 ## A unicorn's partner won't always operate from a place of love and abundance.

That's okay as long as she or he recognizes that and recalibrates. That Unicorn is equally conscious of this fact. No one's perfect. You may not be partnered with a unicorn. We choose who we partner with for all kinds of reasons. And we have to respect where our partner is and remember that they falter just like we do.

The tricky part is not meeting that lack of love and abundance with an equal lack. We have to remember that love begets love. The most critical thing That Unicorn can do when it comes to loving is to keep on loving even when her partner is in a less-than-ideal place. I'm not talking about abuse—that is *never* to be tolerated. I'm talking about when one's partner is not as loving as usual.

If we're lucky, we are partnered with someone who generally operates from a place of love and abundance. When that falters, it can be easy to feel walloped by that lack. The trick is to meet the paucity with love and uncover what's causing the unusual behavior. Usually, when the reveal is made, there is a wound to be healed, and both partners come out all the better for having faced that demon head-on. It may be as simple as a misunderstanding or as big as a simmering issue that has finally come to a boil. Either way, it's always better to have it out in the light where it can be wrestled with.

Being patient is being loving.

That Unicorn knows that one of the most significant components of being loving is being patient. It can also be one of the toughest things to do, especially in a long-term relationship. Being patient is not about "putting up" with things. It's about genuinely feeling calm and generous about your partner's need to do something or way of doing something.

It can be hard to be patient when we've been with someone for a long time. We just want to say, "Stop tapping your foot. You're driving me nuts!" But if tapping his foot makes him calm in the face of stress, we shouldn't only tolerate that behavior, we should feel empathy for his need to perform that particular behavior. It can also be hard to be patient when someone does something in a way that you wouldn't, but we have to be patient with our partner's habits, just like we need them to be patient with ours.

That Unicorn knows that getting frustrated with our partners is generally more about us than about them. Who cares if they took a wrong turn or are taking forever to decide what to eat or are telling that same silly joke again? Loving someone is about being gentle with them and who they really are, warts and all.

 We all need to make our own mistakes in order to learn from them.

That Unicorn knows that loving someone means letting them make their own mistakes. It can be easy to want to direct our partner on how to feel, what to do, how to manage things, what not to think about one thing or another, in the name of protecting them from hurt, particularly when it's hurt that we ourselves have experienced from the same mistake.

Making mistakes is a significant part of living and learning. It's not our place to tell others (even our partner) how to conduct their lives. We can offer them advice and can share information, but ultimately we have to let them make their own choices...even their own mistakes. If we don't, they may forever resent us, thinking things could have been better had we just "allowed" them to do as they liked.

We need to be allowed to make our own mistakes too. It's okay to say, "Thank you for your suggestion. This is what I feel like I need to do." That Unicorn knows she is allowed to make her own decisions and stand by and be prepared to admit she was wrong if they don't work out. Mistakes have gotten a bad rap. There's nothing wrong with falling down; the magic is in what you do once you get back up.

Wanting alone time doesn't mean you don't love someone.

Most unicorns need some degree of solitude. We can only thrive when we are given the time and space to recharge. Feeling like you want time alone shouldn't make you worry that you don't love your partner or that you don't love your partner enough. In fact, if you don't need at least a little space, at least once in a while, you have to wonder if maybe you've lost yourself in the relationship to some degree.

It's vital that you let your partner know that you need that time and why. That Unicorn always does her best to get her needs met without hurting those around her. That goes double when it comes to her partner. Some couples find it helpful to make alone time a regularly scheduled part of their life. That way, both partners get what they need, and no one feels like they're being sidelined by something they weren't prepared for.

And just like you need time, your partner likely does, too. That Unicorn knows it's vital to respect what that time looks like for her partner, just like she wants her partner to do for her. Mornings? Evenings? Inside? Outside? Reading? Walking? However you each like to spend that time—and you can certainly change it up any number of times and any number of ways—allow each other that time and space. In the end, it will make you better able to be genuinely present and ready to be there for each other when you are together.

Love begets love.

People in love should surround themselves with other people who either are in love or support love. People, particularly unicorns, tend to be like sponges: we absorb the world around us. We absorb the vibes, the emotions, the "feel." So it only makes sense that a unicorn who loves love would surround herself with other people (and unicorns!) who feel the same.

If there are toxic individuals or couples in your circle, That Unicorn knows that it's vital to limit the time spent with them. (Or, better yet, eliminate it altogether.) I'm not talking about friends going through a slump in a relationship or following a break-up. I'm talking about couples who always fight or are unkind to one another or singles who continuously lament the fact that, to their minds, "Love sucks."

We are who we hang out with. It's not that complicated. Unicorns know to fill their lives with people who respect their partners and their relationships. They know to surround themselves with people who want their own relationships, as well as their friends' relationships, to grow and thrive. This is about self-care. It's okay to say no to people who aren't good for you. Even when it's hard to break those ties, in the end, you and your love life will be all the better for it.

Our partners are not us.

We all know the old saying that opposites attract. We also know that some similarities in partners are vital. It's obviously much more comfortable to respect the similarities we share with our partner because we are those things, too! But That Unicorn never forgets that her partner is a different person, a whole person, all her or his own.

Being mindful of that difference will help you see things from their perspective when you disagree. "Why doesn't my partner get it?" you may find yourself asking when the two of you aren't aligning. But then you'll remember that they are different from you and that's part of the reason you fell in love with them. Respect the differences, rather than fighting them. Try to understand how those differences are keeping you from seeing eye-to-eye and figure out how you can still come to an agreement despite them.

Maybe your partner's parents always made all the decisions for them, so your wanting to make a decision for them is painful. Perhaps your partner hates classical music or old movies, so hearing either of those puts them in a terrible mood, while you find those things soothing. But, since you know your partner loathes them, why not save them for your alone time or don some headphones? That Unicorn respects what's different, relishes what is the same, and loves how that allows her and her partner to be separate, whole humans in a relationship together.

Your partner's past is important.

We all have pasts. Some of those pasts are lovely, some are dreadful; most are a combination. When you're in a relationship with someone, it makes sense that you don't want to know every intimate detail about their past. That was then, this is now. Learning some parts of their personal history may be hard—divorcing someone they considered their true love, suffering sexual abuse as a kid, losing a child. Some of those things might make you feel like you'll never measure up, you won't be able to help them, or that they'll never heal. But not knowing doesn't always help matters either.

That Unicorn knows that, as with so many other things, striking a balance is key. Listen to what your partner wants to share. Ask questions and then respect when she or he might not want to share. And, most importantly, don't make it about you. Make time for your partner to share without chiming in with your own experience and vice versa.

The one thing we can never change is the past, so we can either respect it or let it control us. Both of you existed before this relationship, and you both still exist as separate, whole humans now. You can tell your partner when you've heard enough about a past love, but do so kindly. And if something is more than you can handle hearing, help your partner find a counselor or someone else who might be able to be the ear she or he needs.

Falling in love with someone's potential rarely works.

That Unicorn lives in the present. Love your partner, not her or his potential. You're in the relationship you're in today, not tomorrow, not next week, and certainly not a year from now. If you want to be with this person, then you have to be with who they are at present. Anything less is unfair to you both.

Sometimes we fall for someone's potential because they are so close to being who we imagine we want to partner with, and maybe they are the closest to that we've ever found. "I can change this or that," you say to yourself. "One day, she'll (fill-in-the-blank), and then everything will be perfect." Could that happen? Sure. Will that happen? Not likely.

We all change and grow as time goes by. But at our core, we remain the same. That Unicorn knows to love wholly and not aspirationally. Doing otherwise will leave you disappointed and likely resentful of the person who never even was—and was never going to be—the person you conjured up in your head. That outfit won't make you any taller, and that partner won't change her stripes.

Love needs space to breathe.

I mean this literally and figuratively. That Unicorn knows to ask for space and to give it. Sometimes you want to be held and snuggled and be as close to your partner as possible. Other times, you want the whole side of the couch to yourself. Both of those are perfectly reasonable. Sometimes you want to finish the puzzle with no one helping. Other times, you want your partner in crime to help you find that last pesky edge piece and figure out where that weird orange section goes.

It's essential that you make it clear to your partner what you need and that you listen to your partner's needs. Sometimes they won't line up, and you'll need to compromise. That is one of That Unicorn's best traits. She knows how to bend without breaking and how to ask her partner for the same consideration.

Take time apart. Have separate hobbies. Take some of your concerns to other friends or family. Don't smother one another. Love is a living, breathing organism, and every living thing needs air to breathe and space in which to move. Establish a balance that works for both of you—that way, both of you are getting your needs met most of the time without either of you feeling like the one who's doing the compromising all of the time.

CHAPTER SEVEN

———

How to BTU When **Traveling**

Traveling can be a bear. Schedules go *off* schedule, equipment breaks, people can be rude. But traveling can be one of life's greatest joys. The key? Why, to be That Unicorn, of course. But you already know that by now. The traveling unicorn accepts the fact that there will be bumps—they are part of the ride. There will be tears...but there's always a tissue. The journey will be worth the turbulence. Let That Unicorn take you on your trips and your trips will always be magical—even the rocky ones.

I used to need everything to go smoothly in order to enjoy a trip. One delay, cancellation, or unplanned detour, and I was flummoxed and ready to bail. Then I started to notice a funny pattern. A delayed flight would lead to a drink at the restaurant, where I'd meet a guy who told me about a restaurant where I could get the best whole fried red snapper in Costa Rica. A wrong turn would lead to a food stall where I had the most delicious falafel you could imagine. A canceled train would lead to an extra day in a city with the most fantastic zoo. You get the idea.

I'm learning to breathe. I realized that the only one I ruin it for is myself, although I'm quite certain I have also made it at the very least unpleasant for those around me. Sometimes that's all it takes to remind me that I am not being very unicorn-y. It's one thing to mess up my own experience; it's quite another to mess up everyone else's. Listen—none of this makes hassles less of a hassle. None of this means you have to be all zippity-doo-dah about debacles. All it means is that, after you've stomped and grumped and sighed, you can either make the most of the mess or let the chaos swallow you. For myself, I don't want to get swallowed up by what ultimately are just #FirstWorldProblems.

I'm learning to enjoy the ride. Yes—I'm learning. Every unicorn is learning. Every unicorn makes a misstep and, yes, even has a moment of regret...but keeps it at another moment. That Unicorn is real. That Unicorn really gets mad, and That Unicorn really gets sad. Sometimes she is even less than pleasant with the ticket-counter guy who is not being his best unicorn self. But she also remembers how lucky she is to travel and how this blip is just that—a blip. Give yourself a break. Losing it is just fine, as long as you don't take too long to find it again.

That Unicorn loves to travel; it doesn't matter whether it's near or far. Unicorns just like the chance to discover what's on the other side of that fence, over the mountain, or across the lake. Things don't always go swimmingly, but when they do go awry, I now let my inner unicorn be my tour guide. Herbert always knows how to turn things around, even when it's pouring rain in a tropical place where the most popular activities require clear skies. (In case you're wondering what the takeaway was from that adventure...bingo can indeed be a drinking game...)

When it comes to traveling, That Unicorn acknowledges that…

Unicorns focus on the end goal.

Traveling is amazing. It can also be amazingly frustrating. A unicorn remembers the "why" when it comes to traveling. Everyone has her or his own why. Maybe it's to see family or friends or to explore somewhere new. Perhaps it is simply to detach from everyday life for a bit. Whatever the why, That Unicorn focuses solely on that, no matter what comes up along the way.

Things will be lost. Flights will be delayed. Trains will be canceled. Any of that could ruin your entire trip unless you keep in mind why you took this journey in the first place. It's interesting how easy it is to get flustered by even the littlest inconvenience when you're traveling. The airport deli that gave you ham instead of turkey. The luggage handler who was less than friendly. The lines for anything and everything that circle the block. But keeping your eye on the prize can help all that melt away.

That Unicorn knows that, despite all the bumps, the real reward—whatever that means—is the only thing that really matters. That Unicorn knows that whatever has to be encountered in the meantime means nothing in the grand scheme of things. That Unicorn knows that, if she can keep the end game in mind, nothing can take the wind out of her sails...even the guy manspreading in the seat next to her...

Unicorns don't get attached.

It can be easy to feel like all is lost when plans simply must change. You have to take a bus instead of a train. You have to hire a car instead of walk. You only have one day in this city and two in the other instead of vice versa. The key to not losing your mind is to stay unattached. It's perfectly reasonable to have a broad overview of how your travels will go. But it's absolutely essential that you remain unattached to the particulars.

Most of our frustrations and disappointments in life relate to being passionately, but needlessly, attached to specific outcomes. We have to get there right at eight o'clock or everything is ruined. I have to buy *that* brand of chocolate or we might as well not go. They have to get us that dinner reservation or this whole meal is pointless. That kind of attitude will most certainly keep you in a state of unnecessarily heightened stress and will most likely leave you devastated when things inevitably don't work out precisely as planned.

Traveling involves a lot of moving parts. Vehicles, people, weather, illness, politics—the list of things that could interrupt your plans is nearly endless. You simply cannot be prepared for every single thing that might happen to your plans along the way. But you can plan for how you will respond. That Unicorn takes a deep breath, allows herself to be irritated, bummed, pissed-off, or whatever for a few moments and then sallies forth. The truth is, the only thing we can control is ourselves, and, more often than not, we are the ones who are ultimately responsible for any unhappiness we may experience when traveling, or otherwise.

Unicorns plan dedicated travel days.

I know this isn't always possible. But whenever you can, having a day to get somewhere and a day to return when nothing else needs to be accomplished can be critical to a happy trip. Thinking you will achieve A, B, and C on your arrival day as well as D, E, and F on your departure day can lead to heaps of disappointment.

There is simply no controlling how things will go on a travel day. If you can't have fully dedicated travel days, consider having at least double the time it should take set aside so that you aren't crushed if (and more likely when) things go awry. That Unicorn always does her best to set herself up for success rather than failure.

Planning a long weekend? Why not drive in on Thursday night instead of Friday morning? Going on a cruise? Find an inexpensive hotel and fly in the day before, so there's a much slimmer chance of you literally missing the boat. Going to Europe to explore for a couple of weeks? Mark the first and last days as strictly for travel. If you get to squeeze something in on those days, great. But if not, you won't have to feel like you missed a thing.

Not everyone is focused on BTU.

Be patient (and kind). This might be the hardest one of all for me. My dream, of course, is to live in a world where everyone focuses on being That Unicorn. I'm not that naïve; I know that, in all too many ways, the opposite is true. That goes double when you're traveling. We cannot control others. We can only control ourselves and our reactions to others. That is my travel mantra.

I try my best to remember that. I try my best to always be That Unicorn. When I am traveling, my resolve is tested more than ever. But if I let myself get upset by others who did not plan ahead, who do not know the rules, who think they are the only people in the world, who think they are the most influential people on planet earth, who think their travel is the most important, it's only me who gets hurt. It's only me who gets stressed-out. And it's only me who can keep that from happening.

That Unicorn is extra patient and extra kind, especially toward those who don't even believe in unicorns. I make sure I have plenty of time so that the lack of planning of others does not affect me. And, if I am affected, I remind myself that getting upset will only result in my being upset. Nothing, not one thing, other than that will change.

There's no reward for going it alone.

I like to do things on my own, in my way. But there's honestly no reward for doing things that way. I can't generally put my luggage in the overhead compartment, carry my bag up the train station steps, or read in any language other than English or Spanish. I could get upset or I can get help.

And you know what's incredible? There is always someone ready, willing, and able to help when you're far from home. Always. I know people who don't like to ask for help when they're traveling. They think it means that they aren't a good or seasoned traveler. Most people don't like to be seen as a novice. You know what? Those people are putting way too

much thought into it and, honestly, they are being more
trouble by holding up the works while they struggle to do
something with which someone could easily help them.

That Unicorn knows what she is and is not capable of, both
on the road and at home sweet home. Unicorns do not mourn
what they can't do or feel entitled or sorry for themselves.
They don't make a "woe is me" nuisance of themselves. They
say, "Can you give me a hand with this?" "Can you tell me
where (fill-in-the-blank) is?" "Can you translate that for
me?" I have never been turned down. A smile goes a long
way, especially when you're far from home, in a world where
kindness is far too scarce a commodity.

Unicorns ask a local.

No one knows about a destination better than
someone who lives there. No matter how many
times you've gone somewhere, no one knows like a local. And
not only is there no shame in asking a local, there's actually
nothing *better* than asking. When you travel, there are almost
always too many sights to see. A local can help you decide
what to see, and how, with the time you have.

Some locals may not be interested in helping a tourist. That
is certainly their prerogative. So ask nicely and don't be
offended if they don't have the time or the inclination. But

most are delighted to share what they know best. One local is likely not enough. If you're lucky, you'll find yourself a foodie and a history buff and a shopping pro in the realm of all things travel.

Asking a local also serves as a sort of bridge. Making a connection with someone from somewhere far from your home can be an inspiring moment for you both. That Unicorn always sheds the best possible light on where she's from and leaves the local with the feeling that her home is a magical place because it is. Think of it as being an ambassador of sorts. Show your respect for the place you're visiting and the people who reside there and what they value most about the place they call home. Believe it or not, there's no higher path to world peace than that.

Unicorns pack light.

You don't need it. Whatever those two or three or ten last things are, you don't need 'em. You can always buy a cheap T-shirt or pick up an umbrella or stop at the drugstore. Unless you're going to the ends of the earth, what you bring will almost always be more than what you really need to bring.

Packing light means you are more mobile. If you can avoid checking a bag when flying, do. If you can avoid giving your bag to the steward to be delivered to your cabin, do. If you can avoid having both hands and your back loaded down, do. You'll be able to move more quickly from place to place and through crowded locations. I know it's not always possible. But, when traveling, less is most definitely more.

The best way to pack light is to plan ahead—on paper. I have a friend who writes everything down from socks to jewelry for each day. If it's not on the list, it doesn't go in the bag. Believe me, you'll be much happier with less stuff to lug around and try to store in a hotel room or ship's cabin or whatever than you will be with that one extra pair of shoes. And, if you really, really need it, you can buy it or borrow it or re-wear it. No one that I know of ever died from having to wear the same socks twice!

Unicorns take it all in.

Most travel goes so quickly and involves so many different things going on all at once, it can be easy to never truly be in the moment. But the point of travel is to genuinely experience every single thing. Take a minute. Take a breath. Put down your phone. Forget about what time it is and look around you. Let all five of your senses out to play. Take a mental picture to carry you through until the end of your days.

Unicorns hope they'll come back to whatever spot they're in again one day. But they're also smart enough to know that that may never happen. So they eat the pizza and take the train ride and spend one extra minute in front of that Picasso and linger just a little longer outside that church. It's all so fleeting. Don't miss it. If you're traveling with others, ask them to help you to take it all in and offer your help to do the same.

The only thing better than experiencing something new or wonderful is experiencing something new or wonderful with someone else, particularly someone you dig. And getting to relive that moment—with that person or even simply with yourself—at a later date is truly divine. Consider writing one another or yourself texts or notes on your phone while you're traveling—"Remember when we stood in La Sagrada Familia bathed in light. That was everything." Life is made up of tiny little moments. Travel is life outside of the norm. That Unicorn savors it.

Getting lost is sometimes better than getting there.

I used to get bent out of shape when I got lost: I'll never find my way back. I'm going to miss the thing I was on my way to see. I'm so stupid. How could I have gotten lost with a map in my hand? But when I was done freaking out and berating myself, I almost always discovered something fantastical that I would have missed if I had not gotten lost.

Barring safety issues (which can arise when you get lost, so resolve those quickly and carefully, of course), getting lost can be an entree into something extraordinary. A gorgeous vista, a tiny café with helpful locals, an off-the-beaten-path museum. Who knows? In the past, I would waste so much time being upset that I would miss the thing I was supposed to find my way to and the unexpected thing right in front of me. A double whammy!

Sometimes getting lost is actually the universe's way of helping us to find something for which we didn't even know we were looking. It can also be how the universe is helping us to slow the heck down. If traveling becomes nothing but buzzing from one location to another, you'll miss everything. You'll miss the chance to see the things that just might change you. And those are the very things that travel really should be about.

10 The best souvenirs are the ones you don't even have to buy.

I have a rule about souvenirs: before I buy anything, I ask myself, "Will it translate?" Sure, that shark tooth anklet seems really snazzy in the South Pacific. But is it going to work at your next downtown soirée in the city or your next downtime moment at home? If the answer is no, or if you hesitate to say yes, skip it.

How about a rock or seashell (where it's legal to remove items, of course)? What about a flyer or a free hotel postcard? How about a photo? What about something that actually reminds you of that moment when you stepped outside of your own life and into another world, rather than something that some marketing person thinks will do that? Do you really need or want a Monet waterlilies paperweight?

And if you do want to purchase something, what about something that will integrate into your life and bring you joy every time you see, use, hear, or wear it, rather than something that will simply take up space you may not even really have to spare? I love to buy a dress or handbag or scarf—something marvelous and unique that I can enjoy for what it is as well as have it as a remembrance of somewhere I once was.

CHAPTER EIGHT

———

How to BTU When **Learning**

Unicorns love to learn. It's kind of our thing. We have lots of questions we want to ask, things we want to discover, and activities we want to try. Being stagnant is not in our DNA. You don't have to be in school to be learning. In fact, if school is the only place a person is learning, we've got a problem. To learn is to be open to and aware of the people and things all around us. In fact, if we look at life as a constant learning opportunity, it can be the most rewarding outlook of all. If we know we don't know everything, we can be open to learning anything. That Unicorn is eternally curious. And curious is exciting and incredibly inviting.

One of my favorite things to do is go outside my comfort zone. It didn't used to be. Not in my bench-sitting days. (See Chapter One.) But now I dig it, and mostly because it offers me the chance to learn new things and to learn in a new way. I read as much as I can get my hands on and watch videos to learn how to do something. I sometimes find it frustrating to have someone explain something to me because I can't fast-forward or rewind. I tend to be an anxious learner. I want to do the thing. I don't want to hear you talking about doing the thing. I'm a hands-on learner and a self-teacher when that's an option. And I am learning to be patient with other ways to learn when it is not.

The unicorn in me is teaching me to expand my learning horizons. There are so many different ways to learn things, and nearly every creature (animals and humans alike) and every experience can teach us something about ourselves, the world, how something works, you name it. We miss out on so much when we act as if we know it all. Know-it-alls are my least favorite kind of person. You can spot them from a mile away. They won't listen to their inner unicorns. They are so insecure that they have to talk about how right they are. Constantly. Folks like that used to make me angry. Now I just feel sorry for them. How sad to miss out on so much because you're scared someone will discover you don't know everything. News flash: none of us know everything, and we never will.

How you learn is a very personal thing. But we can all maximize our capacity and joy for learning by going the way of the unicorn. You can pick out That Unicorn in any situation. Bright-eyed, at full attention, enthusiastic about the adventure at hand...even if it's so far out of her wheelhouse that she can't even see the water, let alone where she's going or see the ball, let alone hit it, if you prefer the baseball version of the metaphor.

(In the expression "out of my wheelhouse," wheelhouse refers to where the wheel is on a small boat and where the navigational equipment also resides on a large boat. It's basically the command center, from which the captain has the best sightlines. When the captain is in her wheelhouse, she's in control and in command. So, your wheelhouse is anywhere you feel the same. Baseball has borrowed the word "wheelhouse" to refer to the part of a batter's strike zone in which he or she is most likely to hit a home run. Think comfort zone. The more you know...)

When learning, That Unicorn acknowledges that...

Groups rule.

Working in groups can be tough. That is particularly the case when someone else creates the group for you. All those group projects where you end up doing all the work and yet every student in the group gets an A? No fun. But when it comes to learning something new, groups are the best. All the better when you get to be in a group of your choosing. Group learning allows you to learn in a variety of ways all at once, as well as teach at the same time. That combo creates the most effective, longest-lasting learning possible.

If there's something you want to learn, the best thing you can do for yourself is to join, or better yet to create, a group. That Unicorn knows that learning with others is the most effective way to learn something because you benefit from all the different learning styles. One person may be a visual learner and so may create and share visual representations of what you're trying to learn, like pictures or charts or videos. Another person might make up a song or rhyme to help you remember the steps to a task. Another might be a pro at outlining and highlighting. You can bring in your learning style, and everyone gets the best of all worlds.

The other benefit of learning in a group is that you will likely get to teach others the parts you already know or have learned. When we teach something, we reinforce our own learning or understanding of something. So I show you that step or stitch or pronunciation or whatever, and it becomes all the more clear and cemented in my brain too. That Unicorn knows that working together can be a challenge but, when it works, it is the most effective way to become a rock star at anything, including maybe even becoming a rock star...

Different things are hard for different people.

This can be hard even for That Unicorn to remember. Something that comes super easy to you may be crazy hard for someone else to grasp and vice versa. It is so incredibly important to understand this, as it can keep you from getting frustrated with yourself and with others.

That Unicorn likes to be good at everything she does. Most people do. So it can be really upsetting when you're learning something new, and everyone seems to be getting it but you. Your first thought might be to quit. But That Unicorn does not quit. That Unicorn knows that it's okay not to get something on the first or second or even hundredth try, regardless of how easy it might seem for everyone else. That Unicorn knows that learning is part of the fun, and there's no shame in continuing to plug away until you master the skill at hand.

Unicorns also want everyone else to be good at the thing because they are empathetic creatures, and they don't like to see other people frustrated, either. Keeping in mind that different things are hard for different people will allow you to be patient while the person learns, as well as help them feel okay about not hitting the ball or knitting an even row or translating a page or climbing a wall or whatever. That Unicorn is kind and encouraging. Always.

People learn differently.

No one learning style is better than another. It's kind of wild how differently we all learn. Some people just have to hear something once. Others have to see it over and over. Some can't do it until they try it themselves. Others have to read and read and read until it sticks. For others, only a song or rhyme will make the info stick. The thing is, the how doesn't matter. It's the learning that counts.

It can be tempting to discount one way of learning and celebrate another. But doing that serves no purpose and can be harmful to the learner and the teacher and anyone witnessing the moment. When we discount how someone learns, we too get the message that there's something wrong with that method, and then we might not try that very thing that could teach us how to do something one day.

By the same token, if we celebrate one specific style, we may find ourselves employing only that style over and over, even if it fails us. We all learn differently, and we can all use a variety of learning styles, depending on what we're learning. You may be able to play piano by ear but need to get your hands dirty to learn how to change a tire. You may be able to sing all the steps to quilting in your head. But you may need to read nearly every line written to learn how to make the perfect macaron. That Unicorn knows it's all good.

It's not just okay to ask, it's ideal.

Somewhere along the line, asking questions got a bad name. That makes me sad. When we're kids, we tend to ask lots of questions, and, hopefully, we get lots of good answers. If we don't, that may keep us from asking questions as we get older. In school, if teachers—or even other students—aren't supportive about question-asking, that too may curb our inquisitive nature.

But That Unicorn knows that asking questions is sometimes the best (or even only) way to learn something. If you have a question, ask. If you're curious about something, ask. Lost? Ask. New to something? Ask. Yes, there is a right time and place and person. But don't feel like you're supposed to somehow be the holder of all knowledge. When I was teaching college writing and my students would ask a question to which I didn't know the answer, I would say, "I don't know, but I know who I can ask to find out."

"I don't know," is always allowed. "Let me ask," is always allowed. That Unicorn isn't afraid to not know everything. No one knows everything. Trust me. And when That Unicorn is learning something new, question-asking is all the more welcome. They say there are no dumb questions. And it's true, because if someone is unsure, then asking isn't dumb. It's moving forward without asking, when you have no clue, that's not so smart.

Memorizing is not learning.

That Unicorn knows that memorizing has its place but also knows that memorizing is memorizing; it is not learning. In all too many ways, school—and more specifically, standardized testing—does us a disservice. We are given information and then tested on memorizing it. But we are not tested on truly knowing or understanding it, which, to my mind, is pointless. Sure, if you're learning how to dive and you need to learn the steps for prepping your tank, you need to memorize them. But you are more likely to remember them if you also learn the why. And you are clearly only going to be able to execute them correctly if you also learn the how.

To learn something is to understand what the things you are memorizing mean, how they fit into a broader context, what uses they serve, and so on. What's the point of memorizing a list of French verbs if you can't conjugate them, and you don't know what they mean or how to pronounce them? That Unicorn knows how to make up a song or rhyme to memorize a list of dates or a group of ideas. But she also knows that that is just the beginning.

If you're learning something just to regurgitate it back up like a parrot, there's virtually no point in doing it. Even if such regurgitation is required, say, for a standardized test, you can still go the extra mile and actually learn about the things you are memorizing. And the secret every unicorn knows is that, the more you learn about the things you are memorizing, the easier it is to remember.

Write it down.

Just because you don't have to write it down doesn't mean you shouldn't write it down. That Unicorn loves to take notes. She has notes about gifts to buy and restaurants to go to and quotes to remember. So it would only make sense that taking notes would be part of how That Unicorn learns.

Writing things down isn't just about having something to refer back to. The actual act of writing something down helps our brains to learn it. So write down those steps to take, those moves to make, and those ingredients to bake. You write them, and you'll remember them.

The goal is to write down what is essential. If we write everything down, we might as well write nothing down, because there is no way on earth we can take it all in. So be mindful of what you're committing to writing. Think of it as a way of locking it in the vault, your brain vault, and you don't want to waste any valuable space!

Revel in your supplies.

One of my favorite parts about going back to school every year was the supplies. The packs of pencils. The stacks of paper. The folders in every color of the rainbow. I thought of them as the reward for all the studying I was about to be buried in. The thing is, I still love all that stuff today.

If you find learning new things particularly challenging, treating yourself to some essential supplies can help ease the pain. They can make learning easier if you get the right ones for the job, and they can make you smile at the very least while you're drudging through.

When the learning is outside of school, it can be especially hard to stay focused. If no one's making you do it, why do it, right? Wrong. Learning new things is one of the best parts of life. And learning things that don't come easily is That Unicorn's stock in trade. The more challenging the process is, the more rewarding it is once you conquer it!

Trust your choice about what to learn.

It seems like there are always people around you who know what's best for you. But That Unicorn knows that only she knows what's best for her. Time and energy and money are all limited commodities. So, as much as many of us would like to learn nearly everything under the sun, we simply can't.

That Unicorn knows to trust her instincts when it comes to what she chooses to learn; that goes for college or grad school, of course. But it also goes for things you might want to learn outside of school or beyond your college years.

Maybe you want to go to cooking school or take an art class. Perhaps you want to learn a craft with the internet as your teacher. That's my favorite part of the internet. There's very little I can't get at least some information about. (Check your sources, of course.)

And anyone who tells you not to learn something new is someone you don't need telling you what to do. Generally, people who think you should stay stagnant are people who are stagnant themselves. Stuck people love to get others stuck, too. That Unicorn knows better than to fall down that rabbit hole. Instead, why not ask them to join you on your next learning adventure?

Don't be afraid to follow your interests.

It's okay to be scared at first when embarking on something new. But don't let the fear of the unknown scare you off from following what calls to you. Don't let others' ideas about that interest scare you off either. Just because some people say girls shouldn't be into bugs, that doesn't mean girls shouldn't be into bugs. It means those people need to get their heads out of their behinds.

Some of your interests may be obscure enough that you have trouble finding the information you need or the class you want. Don't let that scare you off, either. Just because something is hard to learn about doesn't mean it's not worth learning about. Who knows? Maybe you're a pioneer in an underdeveloped field.

That Unicorn always follows her interests. Your inner voice knows what inspires you, what drives you. So just say yes. Be safe and take a buddy. Be sure to read all the instructions. But after you do, say yes. Dig deeper, try it again, take the class, go on the adventure. Feed your unicorn self; That Unicorn is always hungry for all things new.

10 The only failure is not seeking to learn something new.

Chances are you're going to mess up. You won't hit the target. You won't get certified the first time out. You won't lasso it or stitch it or sink it. You'll burn it or lose it or otherwise mangle it. That's fine. That's good, in fact. Unicorns love mistakes because they mean you can try the thing all over again, this time with some experience under your belt.

Sure, you can sit on the bench, keep doing the things you already know, or keep your horizons from expanding one inch further from their current locale. But what's the point? You can't fail if you don't try to learn something new...but you can't succeed, either. No matter how much failing at something new might sting, the sweet taste of victory once you do get it right outweighs that sting every time.

My dad always says, "You can't hit the ball if you don't step up to the plate." I think the metaphor applies here, too. You won't ever get to do the thing if you don't learn to do the thing. So why not give it a whirl? Your pronunciation may never be perfect. Your form may never be worthy of an Olympic team. Your seams may never be as straight as my mom's. But you can say you learned something new, and brain expansion is always its own best reward.

CHAPTER NINE

How to BTU When **Caring**

It's a big word, "caring." It can be about self-care. It can be about parenting. It can be about taking care of an aging parent. It can be about tending your garden. Caring is a big thing. It's a wonderful thing. It also can be an incredibly challenging thing, and it behooves us all to be honest about that.

There really is such a thing as compassion fatigue. Taking care of anyone—including yourself—can be exhausting mentally, physically, and emotionally. The good news is, unicorns are excellent at caring for people and things and not allowing themselves to get swallowed up along the way. Allowing your inner unicorn to be your guide can help put your mind at ease.

Caring is not the easy job that it appears at first glance. You take care of the people and animals and things you love and choose to care for. Why wouldn't it be a marvelous thing on all counts? Easy. Because it's a lot. Just as you require all sorts of care, not only to survive but to thrive, so do others. And when someone can't do it for herself and that responsibility falls on you, it can be hard, no matter how much you adore her.

There's no magic spell for making it easy. Not even for That Unicorn. But there are certainly ways to make it easier, including not letting your own self-care fall by the wayside. You need to sleep and eat and be exposed to fresh air, too.

You are important, too. Just because you're not the little one or the sick one or the aging one or the one with the disability, or even the squeaky wheel who always seems to get the grease, you still need and deserve and have a right to care. Unicorns always remember that they can only be the best caregivers when they first give themselves the best care. It's not selfish. It's survival.

Unicorns love to take care of people. We love to bake for them and make them soup and listen to their worries and make them feel special. We also have a habit of taking on their pain and stress and hurt. No way around it. Most of us unicorns are like little sponges, empathetic to a fault. Then we get overwhelmed and want to take to bed and then we're no good to ourselves or to anyone else. As in everything, your inner unicorn knows the magic balance. You just have to heed That Unicorn's advice even when you feel you want to do it all. She will gently remind you that you can't and you don't have to and you shouldn't.

When caring, That Unicorn acknowledges that...

Caring can be exhausting.

This is a hard one, especially for unicorns. We not only want to do the thing, we want to *want* to do the thing. Of course, we want to take care of people, especially the people we love. But caring can be—is—exhausting. Taking care of someone or something takes a lot out of a person, and admitting that can actually make it a lot easier.

Caretaking is hard enough as it is. But weighing yourself down with guilt for sometimes feeling overwhelmed, or even wanting to quit, just makes matters worse. Moms get tired. Taking care of your parents—even if they are lovely—is a tough gig. Tending to a spouse or partner or significant other can take a lot out of you. It's okay to say that, and it's okay to feel that. And it's okay because it's just plain true.

Once you can accept that it's no bed of roses being a caretaker, you can breathe a little easier. The need for the care won't go away. But the need for you to feel some sort of joy at being overwhelmed by someone else's needs will vanish. Most of us have to do hard things. It's just the way it is. Unicorns forgive themselves for sometimes wanting to throw in the towel. They don't let that stop them from mostly doing their best and sometimes needing to scream into the wind or cry into their pillow.

You don't have to take care of everyone.

It's not your job to take care of everyone. (Unless it is your job, and then you might need to reevaluate your line of work.) When the people around you need to be cared for, it can be difficult, especially for women, to not just jump in. But no one has the bandwidth to take on everyone else's stuff, and That Unicorn knows when to say, "This is more than I can take on."

Sometimes, not taking care of someone is actually kinder because, if your plate is already full, what good would you be to them? But more than that, it's not your responsibility. That's one of the hard parts of being a unicorn; we have a tendency to feel all the feelings, our own and everyone else's, and we have a similar tendency to want to right all the wrongs and fix all the broken people and things. But, as a friend used to say, "It's simply not possible."

It's hard to live in a world where not everyone, or everything, gets the necessary care. Children. Aging parents. People with mental illness. People in poverty. The earth. Stray animals. So cut yourself some slack. Part of being That Unicorn is knowing how much you can shoulder and not walking around with the weight of the world bearing down on you and keeping you from being your best self. Unicorns know their own limits and boundaries and respect them, even when that isn't easy.

People won't always appreciate the care you give.

This one really bums me out. It feels like the one thing that's so fixable, and yet it's so not. Sadly, there are lots of people who are so entitled or oblivious that they simply can't or won't or don't know how to show the appropriate gratitude, which means that you have to do the caretaking you do for no reward. Zero. Not even a simple "thank you."

Parenting and elder care can be thankless gigs and can cause acute cases of compassion fatigue, in part because the only reward is in the doing and the doing is not always rewarding—at all. We do it because we do it. That's it. If you're doing it for appreciation, it's time to either stop doing it or recalibrate. Let me be clear, I don't think this is fair or right. I just know that it's true, and not accepting its truth will lead to nothing short of unhappiness.

We take care of people because we brought them into the world; because they brought us into the world; because we love them; because there's no one else to do it; because we feel compelled to it. These are all perfectly valid reasons. Remember that appreciation, let alone accolades, may never come. That Unicorn is at peace with that.

You don't have to go it alone.

There are certainly instances where there is no one on earth who can help you. But even if it's just virtual emotional support, there is almost always someone out there who can help you, even if in the smallest way. There's no prize for going it alone. If you are in a two-parent household, or even parenting with someone in a separate household, make it clear that parenting responsibilities are to be shared.

If you are caring for your parents and you have siblings, reach out to them. If they can't help in person, then they need to help financially. If they genuinely cannot afford that—which doesn't mean your vacations get sacrificed and theirs do not— then it's their responsibility to research housing and care options for which they can get grants or other funding. They have to help. Period.

It's so easy for a unicorn to just say, "I'll do it. It's okay." But you can't always do it alone, and it's not okay for you to be suffering or drowning in an attempt to do it alone. If there is no other parent or sibling or relative or friend, there are support groups and agencies and places to reach out to. Even if you agree to something at first or have been going at it alone for a long time, that in no way means you have to keep struggling. There is no shame in reaching out and asking for help.

Self-care is care, too.

Unicorns know how vital it is to take care of themselves, too. Just like they say on the airplane, you have to put on your mask first before helping others. If you can't breathe, how on earth can you help anyone else? This is another hard one for unicorns: we think we can just keep plowing through, no matter what. But even unicorns need to be taken care of, even if they have to do it all by themselves.

How you define self-care is up to you. I mean, everyone needs to be rested and hydrated and nourished. Most of us also need time alone, time with others, some kind of movement or exercise, clean and comfy clothes, and the like. But all of us have our own personal self-care needs, and that's okay, too. There is nothing wrong with needing time with your dog, or in nature, or even in front of the television. That Unicorn knows that she never needs to apologize for who she is.

You can't be the best caregiver when you're not allowed to be your best self. There's nothing wrong with making time for yourself, and doing with that time precisely what you wish, and it doesn't matter if no one else on earth understands it. All that matters is that it allows you to take care of those you need to take care of. No explanation, excuses, or rationalizations required.

You can only take care of someone who wants to be taken care of.

This is a hard one. It doesn't really apply to babies or anyone who can't speak to their care. I'm talking about a spouse who won't take her meds, no matter how many times you try to remind her. Or a parent who won't quit smoking when the doctor says it's killing them. Or the sibling who undermines everything you do for them. You simply cannot take care of someone who won't allow you to.

It's hard to accept, and extra hard to watch, and the person needing the care will often try to blame you. But once you've done your best to do what's best, that's all that can be asked of you. This blame-placing often happens with addicts of one sort or another, or with someone who is in denial of their state of health. It seems like a silly saying, but it's true—you can lead a horse to water, but you cannot force it to drink.

You can drive yourself absolutely mad trying to make that mare take a sip. But it will be to no avail. So you offer to care for the person, and if they aren't willing to participate in their part of the care, that is not on you; it's on them. The hardest part for you will be accepting that. So allow me to be the one to free you. It's okay. That Unicorn knows when there is nothing left to do but walk away and say, "I am here when you're ready." My dad says we have to remember that many people won't accept help until they hit rock bottom: their rock bottom, whatever that might be. So, even if a situation is clearly dire to you, that person may not be ready or able to accept care. That's one battle you can't win.

Sometimes the people we take care of will be unkind to us.

It's not okay...but it's also not uncommon. You do not *ever ever ever* have to put up with abuse. If your child or your parent or your spouse or your relative or your friend is abusing you physically or verbally or taking advantage of you in some way, it does not make any difference at all how bad off they are; it is not excusable or acceptable. You can begin by telling them that you will not allow yourself to be treated that way. If it continues, you may have to seek outside help.

This is a dreadful position to be put in, and one that all too often people, especially unicorns, find themselves in because we want to do right by the people who need us. But it's not okay to sacrifice your own well-being, and when we allow someone to abuse or take advantage of us, that will likely never end, as the abuser has no reason to stop.

If you don't feel comfortable with how you're being treated, reach out to someone as soon as you begin feeling that way. The best thing for everyone is to end the abuse before it goes too far. As hard as it will be to do this, it will be worth it. The abuse may well be a result of what the person for whom you are caring is going through, which means they need help—not a punching bag—and you can be the key to getting them the help and support they need, which is likely beyond what you can provide.

We all get to define our own boundaries.

The person being cared for has a right to decide in what way they will be cared for, and the caretaker too has a right to define their boundaries. The person for whom you are caring does not have a right to abuse you. They do, however, have a right to say they are not comfortable with how they are being cared for. By the same token, you don't have to do things that are outside your boundaries.

For example, an aging parent doesn't want a nurse to take them to the bathroom, calling them a "stranger." But you do not feel comfortable doing it. They don't get to call the shots. They get to voice their opinion, and you get to stand your ground. A compromise might be finding a nurse with whom they are comfortable after spending some time together.

Again, it can be easy to feel so sorry for the person in need that you put yourself in terribly uncomfortable positions.

But you have rights, just as the person who needs help does. The goal is to find a compromise with which both of you can live. Sometimes, this isn't possible, and we have to do things that are far outside our comfort zone. When that happens, self-care becomes paramount. That Unicorn is an ace at considering all the possibilities and remembering that she does not come last. She has just as much of a right to comfort and health and happiness as everyone else. There's no reward for suffering.

 Sometimes the most caring thing to do is allow someone else to do the caring.

It may be an incredibly difficult decision, maybe the hardest you'll ever have to make. But you may have to hire a sitter or put your child in daycare or, in extreme cases, in other types of care, if you have a child with special needs that you simply cannot meet. You may have to move your parent to a nursing home because you and your home are simply not equipped to provide the care they need.

It may seem crazy to say, but sometimes it's better for the child or parent or spouse or friend to be taken care of by someone who really can meet their needs. What good is it if you can't work because of caretaking and then lose your place to live? What good is it if your child harms you because he has needs that can only be met in a live-in situation? What good is it if your spouse continues to drink and gamble your life savings away when a rehab center can, not just care for him, but actually help him find a way out?

If caretaking is creating more problems than it's solving or creating new ones by solving the old ones, it's time to look outside yourself. You are not a failure for not being able to manage what is going on without outside help, even when a person you love is involved. Doing our best is all that is required. Erasing ourselves or our lives as we know them is not. The people who love us would not want that for us. That I know.

10 Guilt is a dangerous game that no one wins.

You may feel guilty about not being what you consider to be the perfect caretaker. You may feel guilty about feeling exhausted or angry. You may feel guilty that it feels like the time has come for someone else to be the primary, if not sole, caretaker. You may feel guilty asking for help. You may feel all of these things or some of these things or completely other things. Any and all of it is perfectly normal and patently unhelpful. I'm not suggesting you can simply turn off the guilt. I am suggesting that you will ultimately need to do that.

Guilt is normal. But it is not helpful. And, in this case, if you have done your unicorn best, you have absolutely no reason to feel guilty. My guess is that you already went above and beyond. You already did more than you imagined you could or was expected of you. You already did a fantastic job of caretaking, and the guilt is an all-too-familiar feeling for you and your overachieving self. You feel guilty because you didn't do it all without breaking a sweat or shedding a tear or wishing you were anywhere else but there. It won't be easy, but you have to let that go.

Not that you need it from me, but in case you simply need it from someone, I am giving you permission to release yourself from that guilt. And if someone else is doing or saying things to make you feel that way, you have to remember that no one can actually make us feel guilty except ourselves. There is no crime in saying mercy. Your inner unicorn knows when to call it and will hold you up until the guilt subsides.

CHAPTER TEN

How to Be That Unicorn

You've read all the words and you know all the ideals that That Unicorn holds dear. So what's a unicorn to do now? Well, that, my unicorn friend, is up to you. This book, this life, all the love I poured into these pages is for you. Consider this your guidebook. Pull it out every day. Pick one chapter to focus on for a week, a month, a year. Heck, pick one mantra on which to focus. Decide what you really want. What controls are you ready to relinquish? What attachments are you ready to set free? What abundances are you ready to receive? You have to get to unicorning. I can lead you there. But you have to take the leap yourself.

This a ride that you have to get on, the Kool-Aid you have to drink, the gym you joined and now actually have to go to, the weekly meeting you have to attend. You have to believe and you have to take a blind leap of faith. This stuff works. If you are willing to commit to being That Unicorn, you *will be That Unicorn*. Without you even seeing it happening, it will happen. You will feel the ease and see the path and get the job and find your lobster and be your unicorn best.

With every challenge, you have to ask yourself, "What would That Unicorn do?" Then you have to take the leap and trust that the process will get you there. First, find your magic. What is the special extra *oomph* that you can sprinkle onto the situation at hand? Second, live your truth. What is your truth—not *the* truth, *your* truth? What is your truth, and how can you live that out honestly in this moment? Finally, share your shine. How can you share—with yourself, with the universe, with the people around you—that special thing, that magic, that shine?

My mom says I'm teaching her to be That Unicorn. She is an artist. She won't tell you that. But we're working on her unicorn journey. So until she can say it, and believe it, I say it to her. I tell her how much I truly love her work and how good I think it is. What I am not doing is blowing a bunch of smoke up her bum. I'm not telling her she should get an agent or book a show in a gallery or start selling her work for six figures. My mother is a very good artist. Far better than many. So I tell her the truth, so she can live her truth. It's impossible to live your truth if you don't first wrestle with what that is, the shiny parts and the not-so-shiny parts as well.

People say the truth hurts. But maybe that's because we're looking at it from the wrong angle. My mother shouldn't be hurt by the fact that I don't tell her that I imagine her work ending up in the Guggenheim. I do tell her that her work is art. Those pieces that she claims are unfinished or "simply practices," are actually paintings. That truth actually helps. It helps her see just how wonderful her work is and sets up reasonable expectations. Her work absolutely belongs in a local show or on the walls of friends' homes, not to mention on her own walls.

She has paintings all around her studio. Sometimes she hangs
them around her home. When I visit her, I help her frame
and hang them. I like to dig through the stacks and swap
pieces in and out of the frames and connect the eyehooks
and string the wire and hammer the nails into the wall. I find
it deliciously satisfying to watch her see pieces she thought
nothing of coming to life on the wall. At first she fights me,
teasingly of course: "Those aren't finished. I was going to use
that as scrap paper. My painting friends are going to think
I've lost my mind. I hope my teacher never comes to visit."

But I keep on keeping on. I model good unicorn behavior. My
mother's magic is that she can paint. Her truth is that she's
quite good. And sharing her shine means hanging that work
up and not giving two hoots what anyone else thinks about
it. So I hang the work despite her protests and insist that
she call them paintings and make her see herself. One day,
I hope she won't need me to do that—that she'll be able to
do it for herself. But first, I just ask her to trust the process.
She will feel that way one day. She will see herself as an artist
without faltering and she'll see the value of her work. She just
has to trust.

It can be hard to become That Unicorn—hard to trust, hard
to feel calm and safe and secure in the belief that, one day,
being That Unicorn will come naturally. The steps will be
second nature. And the joy you get from living your magical
truth honestly and letting it shine will feel like home to

you. Unfortunately, I can't come to your house and be your unicorn guide. That's why I wrote this book. Let my words nudge you to your own unicornhood. And think of my mom. For her, those paintings are real. For you, let them be a metaphor for how you want to honor the best in you.

So, here are ten rules of engagement for your pursuit of becoming That Unicorn.

Make it your own.

This is your unicorn journey. How you unicorn is up to you. And only if you do it your way can you truly become That Unicorn. So listen to your inner unicorn about what it is that you truly want and need and what feels authentic for you. Drowning out the noise is one of the most crucial steps in actualizing a unicorn life. A unicorn life is full of contradictions. You don't have to have the partner or job or house or whatever that the world keeps saying you "should" have. In fact, it's high time you stopped allowing the world to should all over you. All you have to have and do is what is truly best for you.

Seat in the saddle.

My writing mentor used to say that the key to being a successful writer is "butt in chair." If you put in the time, if you write down the words, if you work at your craft, the writing will get done. Otherwise...well, it won't. Your unicorn journey is the same. If you want to be That Unicorn, you have to practice being That Unicorn. You have to invest yourself in the process. You'll get out of this what you put into it. It's a lot like that gym membership: paying every month will get you in the door; only working out consistently will result in the health and strength and wellness for which you likely signed up for that membership in the first place.

Finish each step.

You'll know when it's time for the next one. You get to go at your own pace. You don't have to make yourself crazy trying to be all the things at all times. Focus on what is most important to you and, when you feel you have mastered that step, then you'll be ready for the next. Be patient with yourself. You can do this. And a year from now whether you are closer to being That Unicorn or not. So why not go for it? Why not live your best life and be your best you and focus your heart and your head on being That Unicorn?

Ask yourself: What would That Unicorn do?

That's the question of the hour. In fact, that should be the question of the moment, whatever that moment might be. What would That Unicorn do? How would That Unicorn handle the situation in which you have found yourself? How would That Unicorn act with love and abundance while still exercising self-care, respecting herself and anyone else that is a part of the equation? You know. Inside your heart and your head, you know. If you don't yet, this guide will teach you. And, in a snap, you'll hardly need to ask the question anymore. Your brain—and your heart—will ask and answer for you, and you'll know just what to do.

Share your journey.

Most everything is easier and more enjoyable when we share it with others. Let your friends and family know what your goals are, and invite them to share theirs with you as well. Becoming That Unicorn will become second nature so much faster if you have others on a similar journey—or at least supporting your journey—by your side. You can share your successes and failures with one another. You can celebrate and recalibrate together. You can find security and stillness when the journey feels overwhelming, which, at points, it certainly can. The ability and willingness to share is one of That Unicorn's greatest gifts.

Don't be afraid to ask for directions.

The journey to being That Unicorn is not some sort of test in knowing something you can't possibly know. So ask for help when you need it. Talk things through with people you trust. Educate yourself about those things you know little or nothing about. Confirm with reliable sources that what you are doing is indeed the right thing, that it remains true to the unicorn path, that you are doing your best and acting from a place of love and abundance and respecting yourself and others, that you are finding your magic, living your truth, and sharing your shine. Sometimes we don't know the answer. But we must always know that the answer is out there, if we will just take the time and effort to seek it out.

Check your work.

If it seems like you're off course, there's nothing wrong with recalibrating. There's no reason to push forward blindly without checking in with yourself. Doing that could lead you to stray off course and make it that much harder for you to move forward in your journey. Check in with yourself. Do you feel good about what you're doing? Do you feel safe? Do you feel respected? How are others around you feeling? Are you doing your best? Are you being your best? Are you remaining true to the unicorn creed? If not, that's okay—no need to punish yourself. A little regrouping is in order, and then you can be back on your merry way.

Care for your inner unicorn.

Caring for your inner unicorn is vital. Don't let anyone dim your sparkle. If anyone seems dead-set on just that, it's time for a talk. And if that doesn't work, it's best to lessen or eliminate your time with that person. I know that seems harsh. But being That Unicorn is a full-time job as it is. No need to have anyone who makes it any harder for you taking up valuable time and space in your life. Take time for self-care. Being That Unicorn can take a lot out of you. You are a wonderful person. That doesn't mean you don't get frightened or sad or overwhelmed. So take the time and space you need when you need it. A unicorn needs to be whole in order to do her or his best unicorning.

Own it.

This is your journey. You're allowed your journey. No one has a right to knock you; you're on your chosen path. Some people may find all this quite silly and woo-woo. "What on earth is all of this unicorn nonsense? You have to take care of *numero uno* and that's you! Forget being That Unicorn. You're just you and that's all you'll ever be." Here's what I have to say to that: That's malarkey. This is your journey. You deserve to be your best, and you are allowed to take this journey because you deserve it. As crazy as it may seem, there's not a thing in the world wrong with looking in the mirror as often as you need to and reminding yourself to find your magic, live your truth, and share your shine. You are worthy of everything the universe has in store for you.

10 Enjoy the ride.

Life should be fun. Not all of it. Not every minute. Not every second. Not every job or relationship or experience. But the overall journey should fill you with joy. If it's not, well, then you likely are not on your unicorn path. You're not listening to your inner unicorn. You're not honoring the magic, your magic. I've said it before and I'll say it again, we can't all be millionaires or movie stars or princesses. Most of us are just good people, nice people, special people who are no more or less special than all the other people around us. What we all can be, however, is our very best, and we can bring out the very best in others.

Diamond rings and mansions in the hills and fancy cars may seem better than that. But they aren't. They come with strings that could entangle all the stars in the sky. But being That Unicorn does not. In fact, it will set you free and grant you what we all must seek: joy...unbridled joy.

EPILOGUE

———

Think of this book as your training unicorn—like extra wheels on a bike. You get on the unicorn. You choose your path. You take your journey. And when you get to the end—just like the Scarecrow, the Tin Man, the Lion, and Dorothy herself—you will discover you had everything you needed inside yourself all along. You will realize you already are your very own unicorn, able to give yourself the guidance and strength and support you need.

Not that you can't refer to this guide any time you like. And I hope you will. A good reminder is always a good idea. But my hope for you is that this little push in the right direction will work so well for you that you'll keep it at your side as a sign, a symbol of your journey, of all that you are and all that you have come to be. And I hope you'll feel inspired to share it with a friend.

As much as unicorns love to find their magic and live their truth, what they love more than anything is to share their shine, because that's when things get really good. Just imagine everyone on a unicorn journey, everyone being their unicorn best, everyone acting with love and operating from abundance and practicing gratitude. It's a tall order, I know. But this little unicorn has always been known for dreaming big.

The unicorn journey is one that doesn't ever end. It has its magical turning point when you come to accept that you are your own unicorn. And you are That Unicorn. But truly being That Unicorn is an ongoing process. Don't focus on completing it. Focus on being it—on being That Unicorn. And while you're doing the work and taking the journey and working the process, know that there is a whole prancing herd of unicorns right there beside you. I'm here beside you. And Herbert is too, cheering you on every step of the way.

It's time we started thinking of life not as a bunch of years spent trying to be better than anyone else or trying to collect the most things but instead as a gift, a chance we're given to, well, sparkle. That is, to be our very best and to make everyone around us feel like they can be their very best, too.

So, here we go. Let's do it. Let's get unicorning. Let's start leaving a little sparkle wherever we go. The time is now and it's yours for the taking. Let's all commit to being That Unicorn. All you have to do is—

Find your magic, live your truth, and share your shine...

ACKNOWLEDGMENTS

——

Thank you to Papa Herbie for always being my unicorn.

Thank you to my wife for supporting me and putting up with my eternal procrastination and unpredictable and creative way of working and living.

Thank you to my daughter Hannah, who said she thinks this book will be "the one" and that she'll keep a copy on her coffee table.

Thank you to my dad for a lifetime of wise words.

Thank you to my mom for being a first reader and helping me through the blocks.

Thank you to Arnold Wayne Jones, who has always been the very best editor of my words. Thank you for knowing what I meant and making sure everyone else would too, even when I wasn't so sure myself.

Thank you to suzanne l. vinson for bringing Herbie the unicorn to life in watercolor.

Thank you to Charyn Pfeuffer for being a first reader and an incredible cheerleader of my work and for telling me that reading it made her want to prance.

Thank you to Chad Cornwall for being a first reader and reminding me that boys can absolutely be unicorns, too.

Thank you to David Odom Harris for always straightening my horn, brushing my mane, and reminding me what's really important on this all-too-short ride called life.

Thank you to Michael Goles for never letting time or distance get between us and being more of a support in this endeavor than he could ever know.

Thank you to my editor, Brenda Knight, who believed in this little unicorn right out of the stable.

Thanks to the entire team at Mango Publishing.

Thank you to Chris Hodgkinson for the incredible proofreading and line editing. You are my detail hero.

Thank you to Charlotte Morgan and the Nimrod Writer women who made me the writer I am today.

Thank you to Sally Doud, my college English professor, who made me fall in deeper in love with reading and writing when I could not have imagined that was possible.

ABOUT THE AUTHOR

Jenny Block began her career in words teaching college English in Virginia. Before too long, she found herself writing articles and books about everything from art to rock climbing to finding love. After that came radio and television appearances, as well as speaking engagements at universities, at museums, and even on cruise ships. She has traveled the world and has had the pleasure of meeting and working with all kinds of people from all kinds of places doing all kinds of things. That's when she discovered her magic—bringing out That Unicorn in all of us. Now Jenny spends her time and her words living her truth and sharing her shine on a lake in Nowhere, Texas, with her wife Robin and her Chihuahua-terrier Walter.

Mango Publishing, established in 2014, publishes an eclectic list of books by diverse authors—both new and established voices—on topics ranging from business, personal growth, women's empowerment, LGBTQ studies, health, and spirituality to history, popular culture, time management, decluttering, lifestyle, mental wellness, aging, and sustainable living. We were recently named 2019's #1 fastest growing independent publisher by *Publishers Weekly*. Our success is driven by our main goal, which is to publish high quality books that will entertain readers as well as make a positive difference in their lives.

Our readers are our most important resource; we value your input, suggestions, and ideas. We'd love to hear from you—after all, we are publishing books for you!

Please stay in touch with us and follow us at:

Facebook: Mango Publishing
Twitter: @MangoPublishing
Instagram: @MangoPublishing
LinkedIn: Mango Publishing
Pinterest: Mango Publishing

Sign up for our newsletter at www.mangopublishinggroup.com and receive a free book!

Join us on Mango's journey to reinvent publishing, one book at a time.